Stability and Variation in Hopi Song

Stability and Variation in Hopi Song

George List

American Philosophical Society
Independence Square • Philadelphia

Memoirs of the
American Philosophical Society
Held at Philadelphia
For Promoting Useful Knowledge
Volume 204

Library of Congress Catalog Card No. 92-73156
International Standard Book No: 0-87169-204-X
  US ISSN: 0065-9738

Cover photo: from Archives of the Library -- American Philosophical Society.
Hopi man.

In memory of Ned and Norma Nayatewa

Table of Contents

List of Figures   p. vii

Acknowledgments   p. ix

Chapter 1 Introduction   p. 1
   1.1. The Problem   p. 1
   1.2. The Hopi   p. 1
   1.3. The Fieldwork   p. 2
   1.4. The Corpus Studied   p. 2
   1.5. Previous Related Studies   p. 3

Chapter 2. Transcription, Translation, and Analysis   p. 5
   2.1. Transcription of the Music   p. 5
      2.1.1. Hopi Melodic Concepts   p. 5
      2.1.2. Pitch Band Notation   p. 6
      2.1.3. Segmentation of the Songs   p. 8
      2.1.4. The Process of Transcription   p. 10
      2.1.5. Analysis of the Melodic Contours   p. 13
   2.2. Transcription and Translation of the Texts   p. 14
      2.2.1. Recording the Song Texts and Translations in the Field   p. 14
      2.2.2. Working with the Linguists   p. 15
      2.2.3. Third Mesa Variant of the Kachina Dance Song   p. 16
      2.2.4. Modification of Phones When Sung   p. 16
      2.2.5. Summation of Contributions to Texts and Translations   p. 17
      2.2.6. Pronunciation and Orthography   p. 17
      2.2.7. The Glottal Stop   p. 17
   2.3. Extension of the Concept of Breath Accent   p. 18
   2.4. Establishing a Frequency Norm   p. 18

Chapter 3. The Kachina Dance Song   p. 21
   3.1. The Kachina Dances   p. 21
   3.2. The Composition of the Kachina Dance Songs   p. 22
   3.3. The Barefoot Long-Haired Kachina   p. 22
   3.4. Corpus of Recordings to be Studied   p. 23
   3.5. The Spoken Texts and Translations   p. 23
   3.6. Comparison of the Two Spoken Versions of the Text   p. 26
      3.6.1. Comparison of Words or Free Forms   p. 26
         3.6.1a. Substitution   p. 26
         3.6.1b. Transposition   p. 26
         3.6.1c. Omission/Addition   p. 26
      3.6.2. Comparison of Phones   p. 26
         3.6.2a. Substitution   p. 26
         3.6.2b. Elision/Addition   p. 27
         3.6.2c. Substitution or Elision/Addition   p. 27
   3.7. The Sung Performances   p. 27
   3.8. Analysis of the Music   p. 44
      3.8.1. Comparison of the Melodic Contours   p. 44
      3.8.2. Comparison of Pitch Levels   p. 47
      3.8.3. Change of Pitch Level Between Segments   p. 51
      3.8.4. General Maintenance of Pitch Level   p. 53
      3.8.5. Duration Aspects   p. 54
   3.9. Comparison of the Sung Texts   p. 56

3.10. Analysis of the Meaningful Portions of the Texts   p. 56
    3.10.1. Comparison of Words or Free Forms   p. 56
    3.10.2. Non-Phonemic Variation of the Meaningful Texts   p. 57
        3.10.2a. Substitutions   p. 58
        3.10.2b. Elisions   p. 63
        3.10.2c. Combining Substitutions and Elisions   p. 64
        3.10.2d. Additions   p. 64
    3.10.3. The Lexically Meaningless Phones   p. 65
        3.10.3a. Breath Accents   p. 65
        3.10.3b. Non-symbolic Vocables   p. 69
        3.10.3c. Symbolic Vocables   p. 74

Chapter 4. The Lullaby   p. 77
    4.1. Singing the Child to Sleep   p. 77
    4.2. Corpus of Recordings to be Studied   p. 77
    4.3. The Spoken Texts and Translations   p. 77
    4.4. The Sung Performances   p. 77
    4.5. Comparison of the Melodies   p. 90
    4.6. The Sung Texts   p. 90
    4.7. Comparison of the Sung Texts   p. 93
        4.7.1. Variation in the Refrain   p. 93
        4.7.2. Variation in the Non-Refrain Portions of the Texts   p. 93

Chapter 5. Stability and Variation   p. 95
    5.1. Variation in Time and Space   p. 95
        5.1.1. In the Kachina Dance Song   p. 95
        5.1.2. In the Lullaby   p. 95
    5.2. Summary Conclusions   p. 96
        5.2.1. Stability and Variation in the Texts   p. 96
        5.2.1.1. In the Kachina Dance Song   p. 96
        5.2.1.2. In the Lullaby   p. 98
        5.2.2. Stability and Variation in the Music   p. 98
        5.2.2.1. Assumptions Made in Transcribing and Analyzing The Music   p. 98
        5.2.2.2. In the Kachina Dance Song   p. 98
        5.2.2.3. In the Lullaby   p. 99
    5.3. Comparison with Song in Our Culture   p. 99

Appendix: Guide to Hopi Pronunciation   p. 101

Bibliography   p. 102

Index   p. 103

Acknowledgments

I gratefully acknowledge the assistance of the following linguists in preparing the texts and translations of the songs found in this volume: Carleton Hodge, Indiana University; P. David Seaman, Northern Arizona University; Jonathan O. Eckstrom, Summer Institute of Linguistics; Douglas Parks, Indiana University American Indian Institute; and Ekkehart Malotki, Northern Arizona University. Details concerning their contributions are found in Chapter 2. Robert Austerlitz of Columbia University and Wick R. Miller of the University of Utah read the completed manuscript and made several valuable suggestions.

I am thankful to the *Journal of the American Musicological Society* for permission to reproduce material from my article, "Hopi Melodic Concepts," and to the *Journal of the Society for Ethnomusicology* for a similar courtesy regarding my article, "Stability and Variation in a Hopi Lullaby." I must also thank P. David Seaman for permission to reproduce material on the pronunciation of Hopi from his *Hopi Dictionary*.

I am indebted to the following graduate students for assistance in carrying forward this project: Roberta Singer; Paulette Gissendanner; Mary Fechner; Marc Satterwhite; and Carlos Fernandez-Gonzalez. Ms. Gissendanner assisted me in the bulk of the writing and research and prepared the initial transcriptions of the songs. Mr. Satterwhite word-processed the final manuscript and prepared the final musical illustrations. They all rendered invaluable services.

I owe gratitude to three agencies for the funding of this project. I received a Grant-in-Aid from the American Philosophical Society, a Retired Faculty Research Grant from the Indiana University Office of Research and Graduate Development, and a Summer Fellowship from the National Endowment for the Humanities. Without the assistance of these agencies this project could not have been completed.

Chapter 1. Introduction

1.1. The Problem

This study attempts to establish the stylistic parameters of song in a particular culture. I wish to determine what is meant when a Hopi man or woman states that two or more performances are those of the same song. To what extent can speech sounds, pitches, and durational values, or the forms of which they are the constituents, differ and the performances still be considered to be those of the same song? Or, to state the matter in reverse, to what extent must they be similar for the performances to be so considered?

In an attempt to answer these questions I have transcribed and compared eight recordings of performances of a particular kachina dance song and 11 recordings of performances of a particular lullaby. I made the majority of these recordings myself on the Hopi Indian Reservation in the summer of 1960. The remaining recordings were made by others at dates ranging from 1903 to 1984. The recordings therefore span a considerable period of time during which Hopi culture was undergoing substantial change. However, music and speech are conservative elements in culture and they were probably less affected by the impingement of the dominant Western culture than other aspects of Hopi society.

1.2. The Hopi

The Hopi are the westernmost group of the Pueblo Indians of the southwestern United States. They live on a high, dry plateau in northern Arizona, and have been a sedentary, agricultural people. To protect themselves against marauding nomadic Indians, from the fourteenth century until recent times they built their villages on high southern spurs of the Great Black Mesa, where they are protected on most sides by cliffs. At the foot of the mesa are springs from which they secured their water and washes where they planted their corn and melons. Since conditions have changed in this century, many Hopi have descended from the mesa tops and formed villages in the valleys and other locations.

Three separated groups of villages are located along the southern rim of the Great Black Mesa. From east to west they are known as First Mesa, Second Mesa, and Third Mesa. At First Mesa three villages are located on a spur: Walpi, Sichomovi, and Hano. There is also one below the Mesa, Polacca. The oldest of these is Walpi, which archeological evidence indicates was founded in the fourteenth century and which is probably the oldest continually occupied site in the United States. Hano was established by a group of Tewa Indians who came to the First Mesa in the eighteenth century from the Tewa pueblo in the Rio Grande Valley. The Hopi were under the control of the Spaniards during part of the eighteenth century but later revolted and resisted further attempts of the Spanish to subdue them.

The Spaniards reconquered the pueblos of the Rio Grande Valley and the group of Tewas which formed the village of Hano migrated to the First Mesa area at the invitation of the Hopi. By the twentieth century the Tewas and Hopi had thoroughly intermarried. At the period during which I made my recordings on the Reservation, in the early 1960s, the inhabitants of Hano seemed to be tri-lingual, speaking Tewa, Hopi, and English, the second with much more fluency than the third. Tewas and Hopi of all ages spoke at least some English at that time.

The Second Mesa area consists of three villages, Mishongnovi, Shipaulovi, and Shungopavi. The oldest village of the Third Mesa, Oraibi, was the site of political and religious conflict early in the century and its inhabitants left the site and founded the villages of New Oraibi (now known as Kiakochomovi), Bakabi, and Hotevilla. During this century one village, Mœnkopi, was established in the valley to the west of the Black Mesa. According to the Hopi themselves, the inhabitants of the three mesa areas speak slightly different dialects of the Hopi language. At the time of my fieldwork the total Hopi population was estimated to be 4,000.

Hopi society was matrilineal and matrilocal. Sexual roles were unusually well balanced. Women owned the houses and tools of production, while men, who worked the fields, had sole control of religious ceremony. Their celebration of ceremony, according to the Hopi view, was requisite for securing rain and assuring the fertility of the crops and thus the continuance of the Hopi as a nation. Many of their rites, such as the bulk of the Powamu ceremony, are celebrated in secret in the kivas, the underground ceremonial chambers. Others, such as the snake dance and the kachina dances, are celebrated in public.

1.3. The Fieldwork

My fieldwork on the Hopi Indian Reservation occupied two summers, those of 1960 and 1963. I
worked primarily in the First Mesa area. In 1960 I
attempted a general survey of the song repertory in
that area; in 1963 I concentrated on the kachina
dance song, its composition, and cultural context.
(For partial reports of the results of these investiga-
tions, see List 1962 and 1968.)

The recordings upon which the greater part of this
study is based were made in 1960. By that date the
Indiana University Archives of Traditional Music, of
which I was the director, already had on deposit
several large collections of Hopi song. They contain
field recordings in the form of wax cylinders and
open reel tapes as well as commercially issued 78-
RPM shellac discs. I studied these collections with
some care before I began to work with the Hopis and
carried tape copies of a selection of the recordings
with me. Among these were some made of men from
Walpi, First Mesa, ca. 1924. The anthropologist, J.
Walter Fewkes, had brought these men to the Grand
Canyon where their songs were recorded. The recordings were then issued as commercial discs by the
Gennet Recording Company of Indiana.

During my fieldwork at the First Mesa in the summer of 1960 I played tape copies of the Gennet
records for a group of older Hopi men. In the discussion which followed it became evident that they
were familiar with the recordings. I was told that
Hopis in the area had had these discs but had played
them so frequently that they had worn out years before. The men were especially fond of a longhaired
kachina dance song which filled one side of one of
the discs. Some of the men listening said that upon
occasion they still sang the song. Later I heard that
the song had been performed at a kachina dance the
previous winter.

New songs are usually composed for each kachina
dance and these songs rarely remain in the repertory.
This song was apparently still remembered because
it had been available in recorded form. These men
also had a personal interest in the recording. They
had known the singer, Kakapti, as well as the composer of the song. Both were deceased. One of the
two men had had a relationship with the composer
which he described as "godson." Upon inquiry I was
told that the song had probably been composed in
1920.

I found it interesting that the men were still singing a song composed by someone they had known
some 35 years before. I wondered how close their

rendition would be to that of the original performance, the recording of which was in my possession.
I therefore arranged for four of these older men to
record the song for me. Two of the men were recorded
twice, the two recordings being made on different
days.

I also had with me a copy of a recording of a
lullaby sung by a man at Oraibi, Third Mesa, in the
period of 1903 to 1905. The original recording had
been made by Natalie Curtis on a wax cylinder.
While interviewing an older Hopi woman, I mentioned this recording, quoted the translation given by
Curtis, and asked her if she knew it. She answered
that everyone knew the lullaby about the black bug.
She sang it for me and I then played back both recordings and asked if hers differed from that made in
Oraibi. She replied that the words she sang were very
much the same but that the melody was a little different. I then recorded her saying the words of the
song.

1.4. The Corpus Studied

Later that summer I recorded two older Hopi
women singing the same lullaby. Each sang the lullaby for me several times and one was recorded on two
different days. This last singer was also recorded
speaking the text.

I now had seven performances of the kachina
dance song, including the one recorded ca. 1924. I
also had nine performances of the lullaby, including
the one recorded in Oraibi in the early 1900s. I
decided that this material could form the basis for a
study in stability and variation in Hopi song. The
kachina dance song is a composed song intended for
use in a particular ritual. The lullaby, on the other
hand, is a traditional song, that is, it forms part of an
inherited repertory, the origins of which are not
known.

It is interesting to note that there seem to be more
Hopi genres of composed song than of traditional
song. In the latter category one finds only the lullabies and children's game songs, the sacred chants
sung in the kivas by men on such holidays as
Powamu, and possibly those sung at the Snake
Dance. Falling within the composed category are
those sung at the many kachina dances, at the social
dances for young people such as the Butterfly and
Rainbow Dances, at women's dances such as the
Basket Dance, and the songs sung by the women as
they grind corn. Thus the kachina dance song and
the lullaby represent two diverse types of Hopi song:

one is composed for and performed at ritual occasion, and the other is traditional and performed for purely secular purposes.

I was able to add an eighth recorded performance of the kachina dance song sung in 1984 by a Hopi man from the Third Mesa area. I was also able to add two performances of the lullaby, one recorded off the Reservation in 1941, and one recorded at Second Mesa in 1956. The 1941 recording is found on a commercial disc of American Indian songs issued by the Library of Congress. It is identified as a Hopi lullaby but there is no further documentation.

I wrote to the collector, Willard Rhodes, who was kind enough to provide the name of the informant and the place and date of recording. Since I wished to establish the home village of the informant I wrote to the Hopi Tribal Council and requested this information. In reply they stated that there was no Hopi of that name. However, there was a Navaho of that name who was known to have sung Hopi songs.

Thus the 1941 performance is of a Hopi lullaby but the singer is a Navaho. This is not an unusual situation. Members of one American Indian tribe often learn songs commonly sung by members of other tribes. The fact that all songs are learned by imitation, and what must be memorized are often vocables, that is, meaningless phones, facilitates the learning of a song in a different language. The Navaho Reservation surrounds the Hopi Reservation, so there is considerable contact between the two tribes.

The performance in question had already been transcribed before I wrote to the Hopi Tribal Council. No melodic or linguistic differences are discernible between the performances of the lullaby by the Navaho and those by the Hopis. This recording is therefore included in this investigation.

1.5. Previous Related Studies

The earliest study of Hopi music of any length or significance is Benjamin Gilman's "Hopi Songs," published in 1908. This was preceded by his study, "Zuni Melodies," in 1891. Gilman deals only with the melodies of the songs, not their texts. In both cases he worked with cylinder recordings of songs made by the anthropologist, J. Walter Fewkes. After transcribing and studying the melodies of the Zuni songs, Gilman arrived at the conclusion that the Zuni were in the process of developing a sense of tonality and scale. In his more extensive study of Hopi song, Gilman employed several methods of transcription,

including that of attempting to establish microtones. After examining these in detail he came to the conclusion that Pueblo music, and Hopi music in particular, is without a scale (Gilman 1891; 1908).

Natalie Curtis offers transcriptions of both words, with translations, and melodies of several Hopi songs in her *The Indians' Book* (Curtis 1907:471-532), and two transcriptions of Hopi lullabies in *The Musical Quarterly* (Curtis 1921:555-56). There is no analysis. Kenneth MacLeish, in his "A Few Hopi Songs from Moenkopi" (1941), offers transcriptions of melodies and texts, with translations, of several songs, including the "Stink-Beetle Lullaby," which is analyzed in Chapter 4. The text of this song is quite close to that offered in this volume. He also offers no analysis of the music, which was transcribed with the help of David P. MacAllester.

Before beginning this work I had published three articles concerning Hopi song. The first deals with musical and cultural change, the second with the Hopi view of the white man's music, and the third with the composition of kachina dance songs (List 1962, 1964, 1968). In the third there are short transcribed excerpts of Hopi melodies in Western notation.

The largest work since that of Gilman is Robert William Rhodes's dissertation, "Selected Hopi Secular Music: Transcription and Analysis" (1973). Rhodes limits his analysis to range, rhythm and meter, and form, so there is very little discussion of pitch. His transcriptions are Western-influenced. He transcribes the phrases of the "The Stinkbug Lullaby," in the form of major triads (Rhodes 1973:43-44). There is considerable discussion of the cultural background of the songs, almost all taken from secondary sources. He reproduces the Curtis transcription of the lullaby and that by MacLeish in an appendix, but makes no attempt to compare them (Rhodes 1973:97-102). In Rhodes's later pamphlet, *Hopi Music and Dance* (1977), he reproduces some of the transcriptions from his dissertation in slightly altered form. The pamphlet is primarily a discussion of the place and function of music in Hopi culture and is fortified by observations made while Rhodes taught music for five years in the Third Mesa Hopi schools. His views differ somewhat from mine concerning the composition of a kachina dance song, the function of clowns at the kachina dance, and the sponsorship of the dance.

The only other important transcriptions of Hopi song texts and their translations are those by Robert Black in his Ph.D. dissertation, "A Content Analysis of 81 Hopi Indian Chants" (1964). However, Black distinguishes between chant and song, both in verbal and musical content. He gives the Hopi words for chanting and singing, *ča?alàw* and *tá?wna*, respectively (Black 1964:xiii).

For further information concerning studies of Hopi songs, see Charlotte J. Frisbie's *Music and Dance Research of Southwestern United States Indians* (1977).

Spoken Hopi, as distinguished from sung Hopi, has been much better studied. However, linguistic studies as thorough as those on other aspects of Hopi culture have only become available recently. I shall mention here only those publications old and recent, which were consulted in the preparation of this work.

Of the early students of Hopi linguistics Benjamin Whorf was the most assiduous. We are indebted to him for the first good-sized Hopi vocabulary (ms. ca. 1934) and much else. The most useful of the early Hopi alphabets is probably that offered by Kennard in his *Little Hopi* (1948). The largest vocabulary preceding the publication of P. David Seaman's *Hopi Dictionary* (1985) is *Hopi Domains* by Charles and Florence Voegelin (1957). Seaman's compendious work was also preceded by an excellent grammar in *Hopi-Raum* (1979) by Ekkehart Malotki. For references to further Hopi linguistic studies, see the bibliography in Seaman's *Dictionary* (Seaman 1985:567-603).

Chapter 2. Transcription, Translation, and Analysis

2.1. Transcription of the Music

2.1.1. Hopi Melodic Concepts

When time permitted when I had returned from the field I began to consider the problems involved in transcribing the melodies of the songs collected. At the time I was concerned only with the melodies of the kachina dance songs. Remembering the difficulties Gilman had experienced in his study (1891; 1908), I thought that graphs of the melodies made by a fundamental analyzer might be of assistance. I therefore sent a copy of the recordings of the seven performances of the kachina dance song to the late Charles Seeger, who was then at UCLA, asking that melographs be made of them. He was kind enough to comply and in January 1962 I received graphs of these recordings made by the Melograph Model B. In the accompanying letter he wrote as follows, "American Indian singing is about as ill-defined in notatable pitches as any we have run into except for Chinese and Japanese art singing" (letter, 3 January 1962).

The melographs received were indeed very complex. I had previously worked with a melograph made from the recording of a Thai song and I had been able to derive notated pitches from the plateaus found in the pitch line produced. Such plateaus were almost completely absent in the melographs made from the recordings of the Hopi kachina dance song. Here there were peaks rather than plateaus. The line continuously moved upward or downward with sudden descents and sharp rises. I could see no means by which these graphs could be translated into the discrete pitches of Western notation.

My study of the melographs convinced me that Gilman was correct in his conclusion that Hopi melodies were without a scale. But if the Hopis do not conceive their melodies in terms of scales, in terms of a series of discrete pitches, how do they conceive them? During my fieldwork I met no Hopi who had studied Western music and had a knowledge of its theoretical concepts. Thus it would have been difficult to discuss the problem with them even if it had occurred to me to do so while I was on the reservation.

During my field work in 1963 I questioned a number of Hopi men concerning the process of composing a kachina dance song. I was told that such a song was always cast in a particular form, the subdivisions of which were identified by specific terms. Other considerations also governed the composition of a kachina dance song. It always began with a particular pattern of pitch, rhythm, and vocables which identified the kachina represented by the dancers. I have termed this the Identificatory Introduction.

The song is also divided into two parts, each beginning in the higher register of the voice with the meaningful text and ending in a low register with a series of vocables. In addition, I was informed that songs composed for a particular kachina dance could be differentiated from each other by their range, that is, by whether they had a wide range, a narrow range, or an intermediate range. This last concept was established by analogy. A ladder with many rungs was associated with a melody with a wide range, one with few rungs with a melody with a narrow range, and a ladder with a medium number of rungs with a melody of intermediate range.

Thus the Hopis do hold some melodic concepts. They differentiate between high pitches and low pitches or, rather, high pitch levels and low pitch levels. They have rather detailed concepts of formal organization, of the relation of one part of the song to another. But what concept controls the rising and falling of pitch levels?

In 1968 I published an article concerning Hopi compositional practices (List 1968). It was illustrated with a few transcribed excerpts from the kachina dance songs. These were given in our common Western notation since I had not as yet developed an alternative system. However, it was in this article that I first suggested that the Hopis may possibly conceive their melodies in terms of contours rather than discrete pitches. I arrived at this hypothesis through the comparison of the Identificatory Introductions of two Heyheya kachina dance songs (List 1968:46). These are reproduced below in Figure 1.

According to my ear the larger interval in the pattern differs in the two performances. In Example A it is a third, in Example B it is a fourth. Yet, according to my Hopi informants, when a particular kachina is

Figure 1. Comparison of the Identificatory Introductions of Two Heyheya Kachina Dance Songs

being represented the same Identificatory Introduction is always sung. From this I infer that when they say, "It is the same," they are referring to the melodic contour of the pattern, and not to exact pitches. The pattern of melodic movement, upward or downward, remains the same, as does the general, but not exact, size of the constituent intervals.

By the time I again returned to the study of Hopi song I had developed a method of contour analysis working with the song melodies of another culture (List 1983:163-64). Since this method is concerned with general pitch relationships, rather than specific intervals, it can also be applied to Hopi melodies. By this time I also had had much more experience working with melographs. I had developed methods of interpreting melographs of the songs of several cultures and I had published excerpts of these songs in which I compared notated transcriptions with melographs made from the same recording (List 1974). Thus I was in a somewhat better position to interpret the graphs made of the kachina dance songs. However, I still found it impossible to translate them into the discrete pitches of the Western notation system.

2.1.2. Pitch Band Notation

To test my hypothesis or inference that the Hopis conceived their melodies as a series of contours rather than as a series of discrete pitches, I needed not only a method of contour analysis but a means of representing the melodies for that purpose. I therefore developed a type of notation that would indicate the contour in some detail but not in discrete pitches. A note written on any line or space of the five-line staff represents a band a whole tone in width. Although I employ no clef, the centers of the band are represented by the lines or spaces of the bass or

treble clefs as designated. In the transcriptions of the kachina dance songs, the staff represents the bass clef. In the transcriptions of the lullabies, the staff represents the treble clef, sounding an octave lower than written (for both men and women).

Thus, when the staff represents the bass clef, a note placed in the top space indicates a G, a $G^{\#}$, a G^{b}, or any fluctuation of pitch within this band. By this means the direction of the melody, rising, falling, or remaining at approximately the same pitch, can be indicated, as can the approximate size of the intervals produced.

In Figure 2, I give the melograph of a section of the kachina dance performances recorded. Both above and below the graph are placed transcriptions of this section of the song in the type of notation just described. In each case I have also given the transcription of the Hopi text.

The upper chart of the melograph indicates pitch, the lower chart amplitude. The melody line in the upper chart represents only the fundamentals, the overtones have been omitted. A pitch guide, consisting of a series of perfect fourths, is given on each side of the pitch chart. In the amplitude chart the higher the line reaches in the vertical axis the greater the volume. The two graphs were produced simultaneously by styli acting upon a sensitized roll of paper. In this case the paper speed was 10 mm/sec. The possible delay in the movement of the styli drawing the lines is 0.1 sec.

The transcription of the Hopi song text is divided into four words or so-called "free forms." These entities are referred to by some linguists as "free forms" rather than "words" since they may combine more than one grammatical function, such as a noun and its modifying possessive pronoun.

Figure 2. Pitch Band Notation and Melograph of Segments D and E

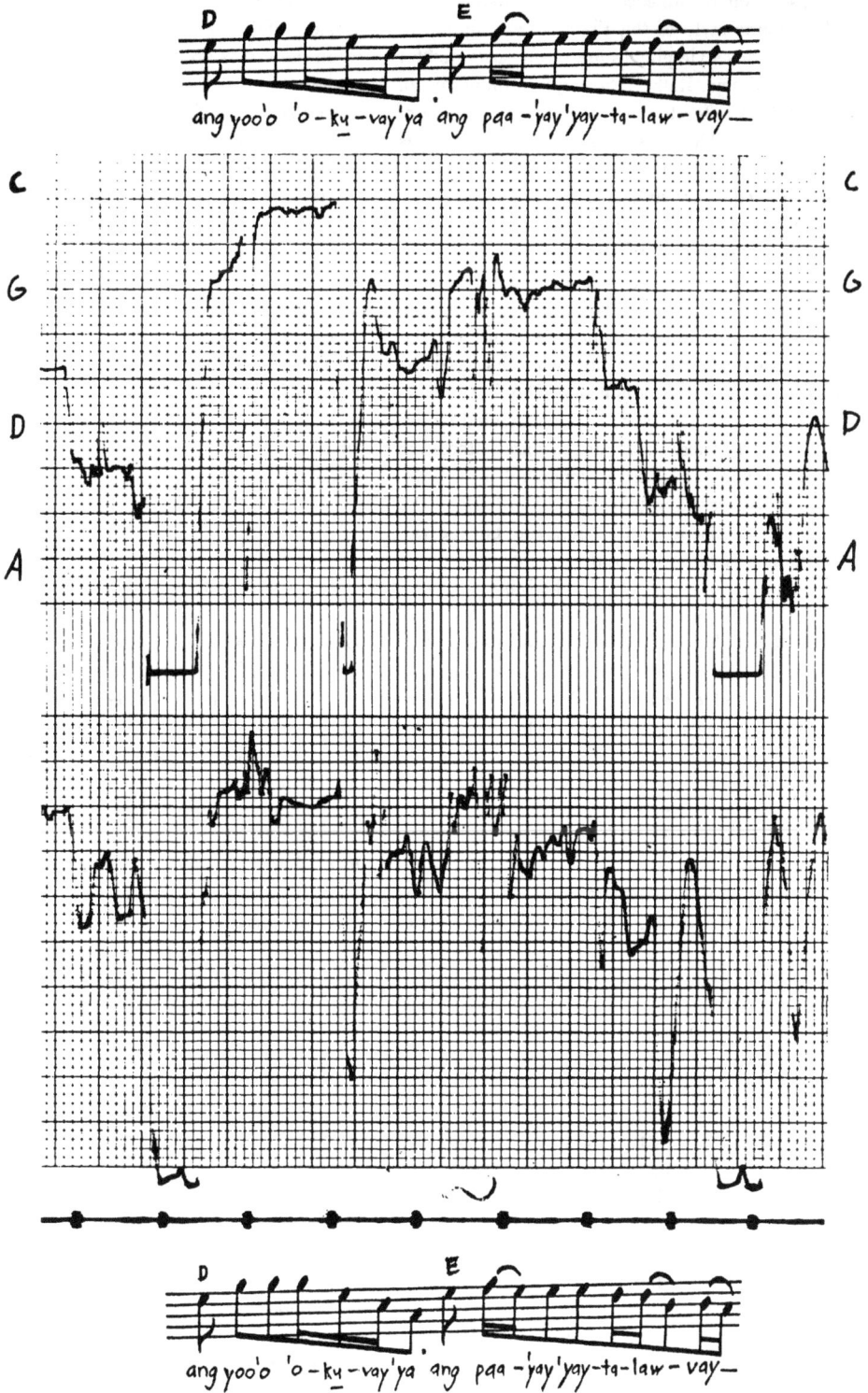

One cause of the instability of pitch in Hopi song is the use of the breath accent. This is characteristic of the singing style of the Plains-Pueblo group of Indians. In this style pitches are rarely sustained for any length of time. Rather, the vowel or diphthong of the syllable is reiterated by a rhythmic movement of the diaphragm. Often, a consonant, such as *y*, is added for reinforcement.

Breath accents are indicated in the song texts by syllables preceded by apostrophes. (In the handwritten musical examples apostrophes are written as short straight vertical lines without heads to distinguish them from raised commas, which represent the glottal stop.) Thus in the second free form the syllable *yoo* is extended by two breath accents and the last syllable of the free form by one. The first syllable of the fourth free form, *paa*, is also extended by two breath accents. These breath accents are reflected in the amplitude chart by crests separated by valleys, the crests representing the onset of syllables. The breath accents also affect the pitch line but the valleys are more shallow or not discernible.

Dynamic accents produced by the same diaphragmatic movement are also applied to syllables other than those which are the extensions of the previous syllable. In both charts it can be seen that such an accent is applied to the first syllable of the fourth free form, *paa*. In this case the accent is strong enough to produce an appoggiatura-like effect in the pitch line. When possible the breath accent seems to be applied to each eighth-note value. In performance this coincides in most cases with the shake of rattles and the movement of the feet.

The pitch line of the upper chart lacks plateaus representing sustained pitches. However, we can consider the approximate pitches to be represented by the crests in the pitch line. These crests can be defined by the valleys found in the amplitude chart when they are not present in the pitch chart.

Following this method the first part of the second free form, *yoo'o'o*, is represented on the staff by the pitch B. The fourth free form, *paa*, plus *'yay'yay*, is represented by G, except for the initial appoggiatura which in the pitch band notation is A. I also hear G as the initial pitch of the first free form, *ang*, before it glides upward to the B. This coincides fairly well with the graph.

The following drop and return, rather faintly indicated by the stylus, must represent the initial *y* of the second free form. The drop and return following *yoo'o'o* represent the consonant *k* and the stylus momentarily touches the pitch G of the following vowel

u. (The *u* is underlined in the sung text because it is a vocable or meaningless phone. It appears in some versions of the kachina dance song but it is not heard when the text is spoken.) The line then glides down to the pitch E, representing the syllable *vay*. After a short rise the pitch line again descends but not far enough to indicate the pitch C which I have written for the breath accent *'ya*.

The third free form, *ang*, is represented by a crest somewhat sharper than the pitch G which I have written. There is then a dip representing the consonant *p* which begins the first syllable of the fourth free form. The pitch outline of this syllable has already been discussed. The next dip obviously represents the consonant *t*, the initial consonant of the next syllable. However, I find it very difficult to make any connection between what my ear hears and what the graph shows for the remainder of this free form.

2.1.3. Segmentation of the Songs

The section of the graph given in Figure 2 is bounded and defined by the breaths taken by the singer. These are indicated by rests and in the graphs by full junctures. In full junctures both the pitch line and the amplitude line drop to the bottom of the graph, remain there momentarily, and then rise again. However, what is seen in the graph and the notation is designated segments D plus E. As previously indicated, I had to divide the song into segments in order to study its contours. Each segment thus represents a contour. The contours are primarily defined by the breaths taken by the singers. However, the singers were not always consistent in the places they chose to breathe. For example, in a second performance of this song the same singer breathed in the middle of the section, thus dividing it into two segments. This is shown in Figure 3.

Once all the performances had been transcribed I dropped the initial segmentation I had made in 1960 for the purpose of securing a systematic recording of the Hopi speech and its translation. Instead I established a more accurate segmentation which is employed throughout this study. In this, the new boundaries of the segments are entirely determined by where the singers breathe in the majority of the performances. In the section of the song given in Figure 3 the majority breathe in the middle of the section as in performance 2Ba. This section is therefore considered to consist of two segments, D and E, each representing a contour.

Figure 3. Disparity in Segmentation

Performance 2Ba

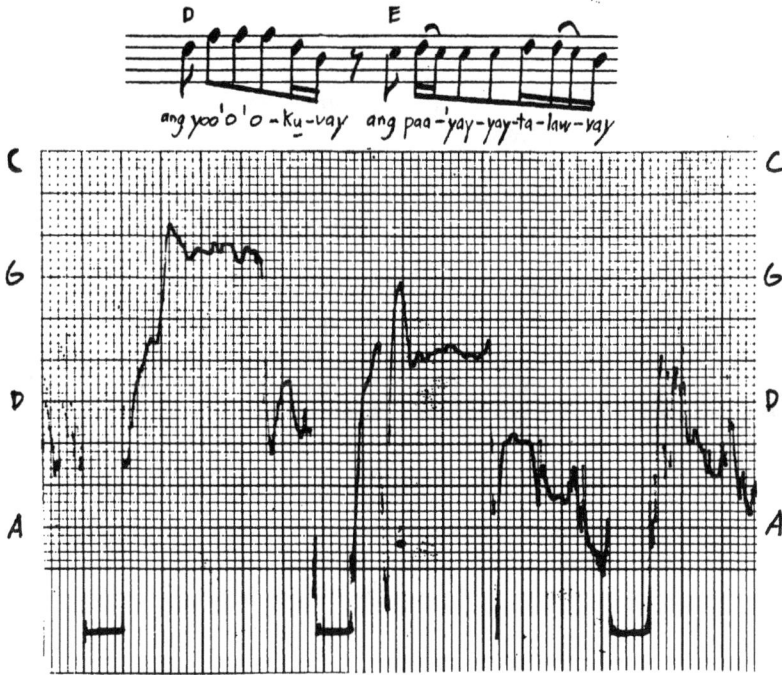

Performance 7B

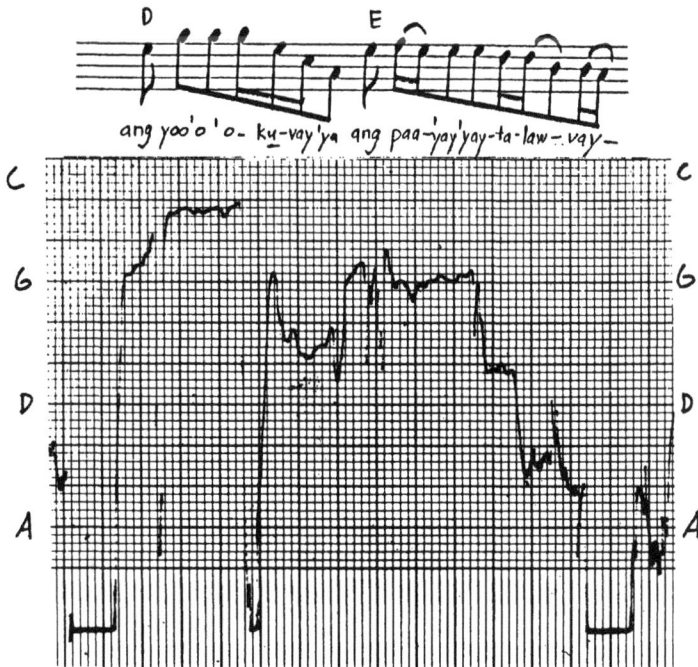

There was little difficulty in establishing the boundaries of the segments or contours in the lull-aby. All singers breathe before and after the three central phrases. The refrains differ in length from one performance to another but their division into segments is easily determined by the longer breaths taken by the singers.

2.1.4. The Process of Transcription

Several steps were involved in establishing the final notated transcriptions of the melodies, which are offered in full in Figures 15 and 56. Working at the piano, I first selected pitches in our equal-tempered scale which seemed to most closely represent what I heard in each segment. I then repeated this process on a different day, often arriving at slightly different results. In the next step I translated the choices made into the diatonic pitches of the pitch band notation and simultaneously worked out the rhythm. In selecting the pitches to be written I had three choices: 1) I could retain the pitch already secured if it were diatonic; 2) I could move it to a pitch a semitone above if that were diatonic; or 3) I could move it to a pitch a semitone below if that were

diatonic. (For my purposes here, I use "diatonic" to refer to notes not modified by accidentals.)

In my analysis of the contours I was interested in establishing a general pitch relationship of a particular contour to the preceding and following contours. The diatonic pitches of the pitch band were therefore chosen in such a manner that the gross intervals occurring between the end of one contour and the beginning of another were maintained, that is, the interval occurring between the last note of one contour and the first note of the succeeding one were no more than a semitone larger or smaller than the interval secured at the piano.

The durational values assigned to the notes making up the kachina dance song were not difficult to establish, since it is a dance song and there is generally an underlying pulse. However, these renditions were not accompanied by the hand and leg rattles which establish a steady pulse at the actual performance. Thus, on occasion, the pulse was not steady and the durational values were a little more difficult to establish. I should point out parenthetically that if the song had been accompanied by these instruments no melographs could have been made. There is no pulse in the lullaby and the durational

Figure 4. Failure of Melograph Stylus

Performance 4D   Performance 3C

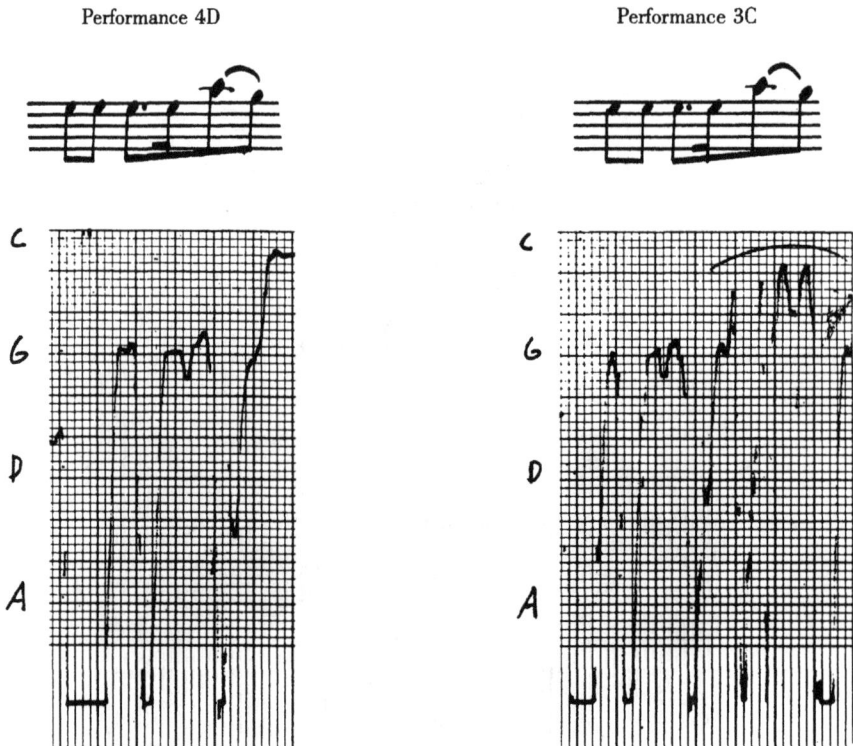

values were derived from an artificial pulse which I established myself. I therefore cannot vouch for the complete accuracy of the durational values written.

As the final step in the transcription of the kachina dance song I re-recorded the performances segment by segment, all performances of a particular segment following each other in order on the tape. Thus one heard all performances of segment A, then all those of segment B, and so on. In this process I not only re-recorded the segment but the last pitch of the preceding segment and the first pitch of the succeeding one. Thus each excerpt began with the last pitch of the preceding segment and ended with the first pitch of the following segment. The notated segments were then compared with each other and with the recordings. I checked so as to be sure that the highest and lowest pitches of each contour and the intervals between the final pitch of one contour and the initial pitch of the subsequent contour were as accurate as possible. When there was doubt concerning the accuracy of the transcriptions the melographs were consulted and were often helpful. They were more useful in establishing the initial and final pitches of the contours than their highest or lowest pitches.

The range of the kachina dance melody is approximately an octave plus a major sixth. In some cases this was apparently too large a range for the melograph to accommodate. This is shown in Figure 4, in which the melograph pitch charts of two performances of Segment Z are compared with the notated transcriptions.

In Figure 4 pitch graphs of performances 4D and 3C are provided with the same pitch guide. The center of the upper square of the graph is indicated as middle C. I have notated this pitch as the highest reached in segment Z. In performance 4D the stylus has no difficulty in reaching this pitch; in performance 3C for some reason it cannot. Nor can it in performance 6C (not shown). In 3C the technician has written a fermata-like mark in the upper square of the graph to indicate that this is "out of range." The melograph behaved in the same manner in the graph made of 6C, a performance by the same singer. In the graph of 6C the technician not only wrote in the fermata but wrote the quoted words above the graph. Why in three tries in performances 3C and 6C the stylus could not reach middle C, I do now know.

Figure 5. Indefinite Pitch Line Below Graph

Performance 6C

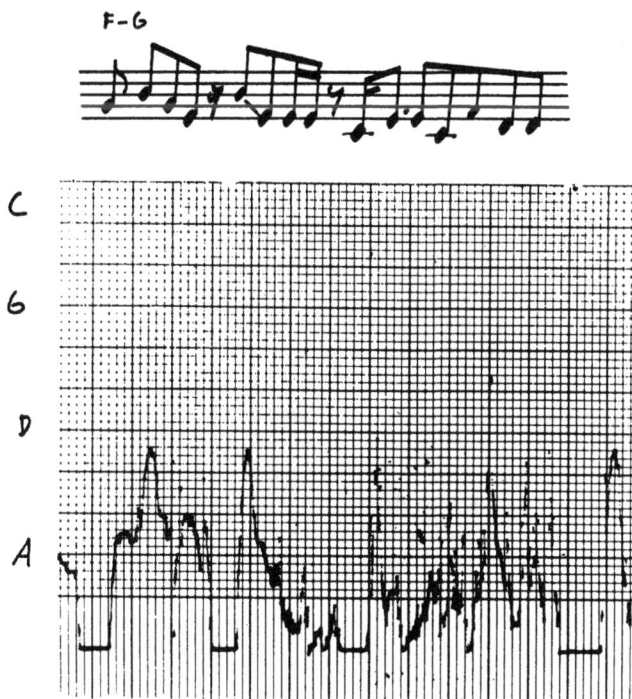

Figure 6. Comparison of Visipitch Derived Transcriptions and Notated Transcriptions

Performance 6K

Performance 11L

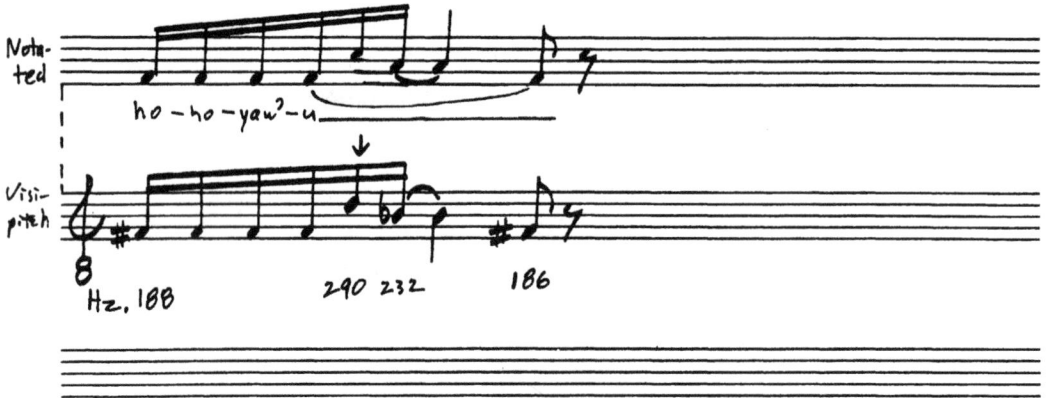

In reproducing the lower tessitura of the voice the line made by the stylus often goes below the graph. In these cases it is difficult to distinguish the pitches produced by means of the graph. This is shown in Figure 5, in which the pitch chart of the melograph and the notated transcription of the segment are compared.

Because of the wide range of the kachina dance song in places like the one illustrated in Figure 5, most of those performing sing below their normal range. Their pitch is therefore indistinct. For this reason what I have written from the lowest line of the bass clef down is often only an educated guess. Singer D, on the other hand, does sing fairly discernible pitches in the low register.

In transcribing the lullaby melodies I followed very much the same process as in working with the kachina dance song. Since the breath accent is only occasionally employed in the lullabies, I assumed I would have no need for graphs made by a fundamental analyzer. However, in some of the performances I found the pitch to be quite unstable. I also discovered that when several singers sang the same contour its widest interval varied by as much as a whole tone. This variation in the size of an interval strengthened my belief that the Hopis conceive their melodies in terms of contours rather than discrete pitches.

I therefore decided it would be useful to check at least part of my results by means of a fundamental analyzer. I recorded in sequence all performances of

Figure 7. Types of Glides

Phrase A of the lullaby. The text of this phrase is *ho-ho-yawꞋ,u*. A Visipitch 6087 in the Indiana University Linguistics Laboratory was then employed in an attempt to establish the exact Hz of each pitch. This apparatus derives the fundamentals from a recorded melodic phrase four or five seconds in length and projects it upon a display screen where the pitch line is frozen. The cursor is focused at the point on the screen whose frequency the operator wishes to determine. The apparatus then supplies a digital readout in Hz on a smaller screen. The work of determining the pitches and their values in Hz in the performances of Phrase A was carried out by my research assistant with the aid of the technician in the Linguistics Laboratory.

In Figure 6 two such comparisons are presented. (Since my transcriptions here are taken from the comparative score [Fig. 56], they sound an octave lower than the equivalent treble-clef notes.)

In the notation realized from the graphs, and in Figure 57, an arrow indicates that the pitch is as much as a quarter tone flat or sharp. The Hz reading for each note derived from the Visipitch is given below the staff.

Comparing my transcriptions of 6K with the notes realized from the Visipitch, it will be seen that the lowest pitch of the first interval is the same in both. However, there is a difference of a semitone between the upper pitch of the two intervals. In the transcription the upper note is an E while it is an F in the realization of the Visipitch. As explained previously (2.1.2), I have considered a deviation of a semitone acceptable in working out the pitch band. Making a similar comparison of the phrase in performance 11L, a difference of a semitone is found in the lower pitch of the two intervals, but of a whole tone in the upper pitch, a C in the transcription and a D in the realized Visipitch notation. Since I have avoided a deviation larger than a semitone in preparing the pitch band notation, this is a case, as in some points in the melographs, where the acoustical evidence and my ear do not agree.

In the pitch band, glides are notated in two manners. In the first type the duration of the glide is given above it in parentheses and the glide ends with a small black note without a stem. This note has no durational value and merely indicates the approximate point at which the glide ends. The second form is standard musical notation for a glide; the glide takes its duration from that of the first note.

2.1.5. Analysis of the Melodic Contours

In the contour analysis I employ the capital letters H, L, and M in general to characterize the melodic contour. H refers to the highest pitch of the contour, whether found in the initial, medial, or final position in the contour. Similarly, L refers to the lowest pitch found in the melodic contour, no matter what its position. M, on the other hand, is a designation which is purely relative in character. It does not refer to a pitch midway between H and L nor to an average or median pitch occurring between H and L. It merely refers to a pitch which is lower than H and higher than L.

M is indicated only when it occurs in initial or final position in the melodic contour. In movements of the melodic lines symbolized by H L or L H, unless the contour consists of only two pitches, there obviously will be a pitch between H and L which could be designated M. However, for purposes of contour analysis it does not seem necessary to give it. The above will be clarified by the examples given in Figure 8.

A melodic contour may arrive at its highest and/or lowest pitch at more than one point within a contour. Each of these points will be indicated by H or L. On the other hand, the designation M is only applied to initial or final pitches of a melodic contour. M will therefore appear not more than twice in any contour.

If there is an M in both initial and final position, and they are unmodified by superscripts, the represent the same pitch. Since M is a purely relative

Figure 8. Examples of Contour Analysis

Figure 9. Further Examples of Contour Analysis

designation it may represent different pitches in initial and final positions. In this case superscripts are added. M^2 represents the higher pitch, M^1 the lower.

The capital letter R represents a contour (or perhaps it might be described as a non-contour) in which the same pitch is repeated throughout the segment.

2.2. Transcription and Translation of the Texts

2.2.1. Recording the Song Texts and Translations in the Field

Since the study concerned songs, I needed transcriptions not only of the melodies but of the sung texts and their translations into English. As a practicing ethnomusicologist I assumed I should find some means of transcribing the melodies of the songs. However, I had a very limited competence as a linguist and I had never before worked with an American Indian language. I expected to secure the assistance of a professional linguist in carrying forward this part of the study. Toward this end I arranged to record Hopis saying the words of the songs and then translating them into English. I began with the recorded performances of the lullabies. For this work I secured the assistance of a Hopi man of middle age who had a fairly good command of English.

The lullaby is very short, consisting of three phrases and a refrain, the latter built up by the repetition of the same word. I had brought with me a copy of Curtis's transcription of this lullaby from her *The Indians' Book* (Curtis 1907:498-99). We were able to use her textual transcription to distinguish one phrase from another. I marked the phrases in the transcription as A, B, and C, and we referred to them as such in our discussion.

Using two tape recorders, I began by re-recording the song sung at Oraibi while my Hopi translator listened. I next requested that he say the words of the song into the microphone connected with the second tape recorder and then to translate them into English. I next asked him to divide the Hopi into what he considered meaningful units, and then to give as good an English equivalent for each as he could. Following this I re-recorded a performance by one of the First Mesa women and we proceeded in the same manner. My Hopi translator declared that the words were exactly the same in the two performances. As we went through the remaining performances which I had recorded that summer, in some cases he found a modifying syllable was omitted and that in others the phrases I had marked A, B, and C were sung in a different order. In one performance the singer added a section sung in vocables, in meaningless syllables. All this was duly recorded, as were the questions I directed at the translator and his answers.

The kachina dance song obviously presented greater problems than the lullaby because of its length and complexity. For the translation of this song I therefore selected a Hopi who had some previous experience in working with a linguist. He was a younger man than my previous translator, spoke both Hopi and Tewa, and had quite fluent English. Before working with my second translator I re-recorded the performance of the kachina dance song by Kakapti and one of the performances I had recorded that summer. In re-recording I broke each performance into segments and announced a letter name before each. In most cases these segments were defined by breaths taken by the singer before and after the segment.

I worked on this material with my second translator for an entire day, following, in general, the procedure I had used in securing translations of the lullaby. However, in this case I re-recorded one identified segment at a time, then asked the translator to say the words and give an English equivalent for each segment. Following this I asked him to break the segment into meaningful units or words and to attempt to offer English equivalents. This done, I proceeded to re-record the succeeding segment. On occasion it was necessary to bridge the segmental boundaries I had established in order to construct a meaningful unit of Hopi. If all or part of what was heard consisted of vocables meaningless in Hopi speech the translator so informed me. We continued in this manner until all segments of both performances had been subjected to this process.

I then spent several days studying what I had recorded and preparing a tentative transcription of the meaningful text of the performance by Kakapti. My translator found only one difference between Kakapti's performance and the one I had recorded earlier in the summer. For this reason it did not seem useful to prepare a transcription and translation of the second performance as well.

During my study of the material I had developed a number of questions. I then had a second session with my translator during which my tentative transcription and translation served as a basis for further discussion. This session was quite lengthy and at its end the resulting corrections of the transcription and translation were recorded.

2.2.2. Working with the Linguists

Having completed the work in the field, I was under the impression that this material would be sufficient to permit an accurate and adequate translation by a linguist. In this I was overly optimistic as the following paragraphs demonstrate.

Unfortunately, linguists normally work with informants, speakers of the language, rather than recordings. When they do work with recordings they need to check their results with an informant and no Hopi informant was available on the Indiana University campus. I also did not realize how few linguists worked with song texts, with language as it is sung rather than spoken. Nevertheless, with the assistance of several linguists and some effort on my own part, I believe I am able to offer here transcriptions of the song texts, both as they would be spoken and as they are sung, as well as translations which are as accurate as could possibly be secured.

The first linguist from whom I solicited aid was Carleton Hodge of Indiana University, who kindly undertook the task of preparing the requested transcription and translations. He worked with the spoken text recorded by my second Hopi translator with only an occasional reference to the sung text. Thus he omitted consideration of vocables and breath accents, only attempting to transcribe the meaningful aspects of the text, and then to prepare a translation.

In the recordings from which Hodge worked the translator had said each segment or free form, as the case may be, several times but not necessarily in the same time period. There was variation in the phones he utilized in saying the same segment or word and this caused difficulties. Hodge had worked briefly with Hopi informants in the past but none was available to him while he was preparing the transcription. He consulted the few works written concerning the Hopi language, such as those by Benjamin Whorf and by Charles and Florence Voegelin, but could not secure sufficient information to prepare a fully accurate transcription and translation of the spoken text of the kachina dance song. Some elements were still in doubt.

Hodge knew that P. David Seaman of the Anthropology Department of Northern Arizona University at Flagstaff was preparing a dictionary of the Hopi language. Hodge advised me to send his transcription and translation of the spoken text of the kachina dance song to Seaman, and ask if he could offer corrections. This I did, and Seaman, with the assistance of Jonathan O. Ekstrom, who was working with him on the dictionary project, was kind enough to offer a few corrections which were incorporated into Hodge's transcription and translation. However, there remained a number of free forms for which there were alternative readings, as well as questions concerning the translation.

Using the corrected transcription of the spoken text as a guide, I endeavored to transcribe the texts of the sung performances of the kachina dance song. In so doing I also transcribed the vocables and breath accents.

I did not find the results I achieved very satisfactory and discontinued further work on the project for the time being. David Seaman had informed me that he would provide me with a computer printout of the Hopi dictionary he was preparing as soon as it was completed. I secured a copy from him in the summer of 1983. With it in hand, I not only endeavored to improve the transcriptions and translations of the kachina dance song but also made my first attempt at transcribing and translating the lullabies.

Soon thereafter I was fortunate enough to secure the assistance of Douglas Parks, a linguist at the Indiana University American Indian Studies Research Institute. Parks was a specialist in the languages of the Indians of the Northern Plains and had never before worked with Hopi. However, he had done some work with song texts and was sympathetic to the aims of my investigation. Utilizing whenever possible the work already accomplished, he attempted to provide me with adequate transcriptions and translations of the spoken text of both the kachina dance song and the lullaby. In this he relied not only on his own knowledge of American Indian languages but referred to Seaman's Dictionary as well as the grammar which had been published by Ekkehart Malotki in *Hopi-Raum* (Malotki 1979). The latter was not known by the linguistic community in Bloomington at the time that Carleton Hodge had worked with me.

Parks was not fully satisfied with his results. Since he had not worked with Hopi speech before he could not be certain of particular phones and constructions. Hearing that Malotki was now on the faculty of Northern Arizona University, Parks suggested that I contact him to see if more definitive results could be achieved. I therefore wrote to Malotki, who proved to be extremely helpful. I sent him a copy of Parks's translation of the spoken text of the lullaby and a cassette with recordings of the songs and asked for his comments. Malotki knew the song and quickly responded not only with corrected transcriptions and translations but with a morphemic analysis of the Hopi. I then made the same request concerning the kachina dance song and after some time received a similar contribution regarding this. Malotki was also kind enough to answer queries for further clarification. However, he did indicate that he worked entirely with Third Mesa informants and that he knew

that in some cases alternative forms were in use in First Mesa.

2.2.3. Third Mesa Variant of the Kachina Dance Song

Malotki pointed out that what I was studying was only part of the song, a fact of which I was aware, and that he had an informant who could record the entire song for me. Having an informant with whom to work, Malotki could then provide me not only with a transcription of the entire song but one which would be more accurate. I made arrangements for this recording and requested that I receive transcriptions not only of the spoken text but of the sung text as well. When this material arrived, I discovered that the song was sung somewhat differently at the Third Mesa and that it would be necessary to give separate transcriptions and translations of the Third Mesa and First Mesa versions. In further correspondence with Malotki I was informed that he had only prepared the spoken version of the song and had asked his informant to prepare the sung version.

2.2.4. Modification of Phones When Sung

By this date Parks had at my request transcribed the sung performances of both the kachina dance song and the lullaby. Of the three linguists who had transcribed the material he was therefore the only one who had been willing to work with the texts as sung. He now assisted me in putting all the transcriptions and translations in the best order possible.

At this point it was I who was not fully satisfied with the results. In most languages words or their constituent phones are often sung differently than they are spoken, that is, speech is modified when it is sung. I was interested in studying the differences which occur when Hopi is sung rather spoken. Parks had noted the elisions made by the singers in taking breaths and other omissions of words or phones. He had also noted some modifications of phones in words when they were sung. However, after many months of careful study of the recordings I heard many more of the latter type of modifications than he. Linguists' primary work is to establish the norms of a language and I was convinced that in some cases Parks was projecting the norms rather than reflecting what was actually sung. We discussed this and after listening to the recordings again he agreed that, at times, for example, the high *e* (like the German [e]) or the phone cluster or diphthong *ey* was substituted in singing for the spoken *i*. He then suggested that I take the responsibility for indicating these types of modifications when I heard them. This I did.

2.2.5. Summation of Contributions to Texts and Translations

Thus the texts of the songs as offered in these pages represent the collaboration of a number of linguists and one ethnomusicologist, as follows:

1. The spoken texts and the translations thereof are almost entirely the work of the linguists. The spoken text and translation of the lullaby were those made by Parks with corrections which he accepted from Malotki. The transcription and translation of the spoken text of the First Mesa version of the kachina dance song represent the combined efforts of three linguists. The initial work was done by Carleton Hodge, and improved by Parks, who then accepted further corrections from Malotki. A few corrections made by Seaman and Ekstrom were incorporated in the Hodge version. Seaman and Malotki should also be credited for contributions made by their dictionary and grammar respectively. (I did not receive a printout of the grammar prepared for Seaman's dictionary until December, 1985, by which time all the transcriptions and translations had been completed. It is my opinion that it would have materially assisted this work had it been available earlier.) The transcription and translation of the spoken text of the Third Mesa kachina dance song are almost entirely the work of Malotki.

2. The meaningful texts of the sung performances of both the lullaby and the kachina dance song, including both First Mesa and Third Mesa versions, were made by Parks and were based primarily on the spoken versions.

3. I am primarily responsible for the transcription of vocables and breath accents in all sung versions. I am also responsible for phonetic modifications seen in the sung text when compared with the spoken text, especially in the substitution of *ey* for *i* and *ay* for *a*. I also supplied the transcriptions of meaningless phones added to words or free forms. The transcription of the Third Mesa version of the sung kachina dance song prepared by Malotki's informant has been discarded. The meaningful part of the sung text was the same as Malotki's spoken text and the added vocables and breath accents are not accurate. Malotki's informant wrote all breath accents as glottal stops, an unlikely occurrence in Hopi (see below). At one point in our correspondence Malotki informed me that he was unacquainted with the concept of

breath accent. The above indicates the difficulties encountered when an individual scholar attempts an inter-disciplinary study and is not fully competent in both disciplines involved. Since few scholars are so equipped, it would seem that such a project should have been initiated as a team investigation. Unfortunately, joint efforts of this kind were uncommon at the time my fieldwork was done.

2.2.6. Pronunciation and Orthography

A pronunciation guide to Hopi is given in an appendix. Nevertheless, it seems wise at this point to offer a few comments concerning pronunciation and, in particular, how the language has been written. For ease in printing the *u* represents the barred i, [*ɨ*], the high, unrounded back vowel. The *s* in Hopi is pronounced somewhere between an *s* and an *sh*. When in the sung texts I heard this sound primarily as *sh* rather than *s*, it is so written. Only one diacritical mark is employed, the umlaut or dieresis over the *o*. The Hopi phone is similar to the *ö* in German. (Seaman uses the slash in the *o* instead, *ø*, as in Danish. Malotki employs the umlaut.)

In Hopi there is a contrast between long and short vowels. In these transcriptions a double vowel has been used to represent a long vowel, and a single vowel to represent the short. Thus *aa* represents the long vowel, *a* the short. Since this contrast is phonemically significant, it is carried over into the sung texts. It is not clear whether the two types of vowels also differ in quality. When a long vowel is found in the spoken text it will be seen in the sung text as well, whether or not it is sung to a pitch longer than a single pulse. (The pulse is represented by an eighth-note value.)

In the transcriptions three phones are employed which are not found in Hopi. The first is the voiceless *l* [*ɬ*], which is used in Zuni. I have also transcribed some phones contained in vocables as *æ* (the *a* in c*a*t), and the schwa [ə] (the sound heard in *a* of *a*but).

2.2.7. The Glottal Stop

In these transcriptions the glottal stop is indicated by a raised comma (ʼ). Linguists commonly represent the glottal stop by the apostrophe but here this indicates the breath accent. In Hopi speech two adjacent vowels which do not form a diphthong must be separated by a glottal stop, as in *hohoyawʼu*. A great number of Hopi words begin and/or end with a diph-

Figure 10. Omission of Glottal Stops Between Words

A   B   C

iyaaha'imöyhoyatu'iyaaha'imömu'umuhkway

iyaaha imöyhoyatu iyaaha imömu umuhkway

thong. When one word ends with a vowel and the following word begins with one, they obviously must be separated by a glottal stop. Since it is expected that most words will be separated by glottal stops, these have been omitted in the transcriptions (see Figure 10). The upper line indicates what is usually spoken, the lower line what has been written. There are two words or free forms in both segments A and B. I have given only the first word of segment C.

Should the glottal stops be written and the spaces between the words preserved, the glottal stop could of course appear following one word or preceding the subsequent word. In one case, in segment S, the glottal stop following the word pu' was so prominent that the linguists wrote it in their spoken versions. At times it can be heard in the sung performances and at other times not.

The glottal stop is particularly difficult to hear in the cases where it is immediately followed by a breath. This is demonstrated in Figure 11, where I give not only the notation and the text of a short section of three performances of the song but also melographs representing these performances. It should be remembered that the upper chart represents pitch and the lower chart amplitude. In 4D, where I wrote both a glottal stop and a sixteenth rest, the line in both cases drops to the bottom of the graph, the pitch chart showing a short trough. In performance 7B the line in the pitch chart barely touches bottom and that of the amplitude chart descends only to midpoint. Here I have written only a glottal stop. In performance 3C the line of the pitch chart drops only halfway and that of the amplitude chart only a little. If the singer had intended to emit a glottal stop, it was not sufficiently audible to register in my ear.

The linguists did not always agree in delineating the boundaries of free forms or words. In one or two cases I have combined free forms in order to achieve consistency in the writing of the several versions.

2.3. Extension of the Concept of Breath Accent

In the process of transcribing the breath accents, I discovered that in the kachina dance songs, at least, a breath accent following a meaningful syllable could occur on a different pitch than the meaningful syllable. This somewhat broadened the concept of "breath accent," as I had previously understood it.

This phenomenon is illustrated in Figure 12 below. In a. the meaningful syllable mö is immediately followed by a breath accent sung at a lower pitch. The second syllable might be considered a vocable rather than a breath accent. I prefer to analyze it as the latter since it contains the same vowel as the syllable which precedes it. In b. the meaningful syllable is first followed by two breath accents on the same pitch and then by a series of breath accents which are sung to two downward slurred pitches as well as single pitches, the whole beginning at a higher level than the first three syllables. This is an excellent example of the extended use of breath accents.

2.4. Establishing a Frequency Norm

Unfortunately, there is no established frequency at which an event must occur in the same manner in order to be considered a norm. In the past I have used a 75 percentile as a measurement of such a norm (List 1963:10-11). Thus, if the event occurs in the same manner three times out of four, I consider it a cultural norm.

Figure 11. Transcription of Glottal Stops in Sung Performances

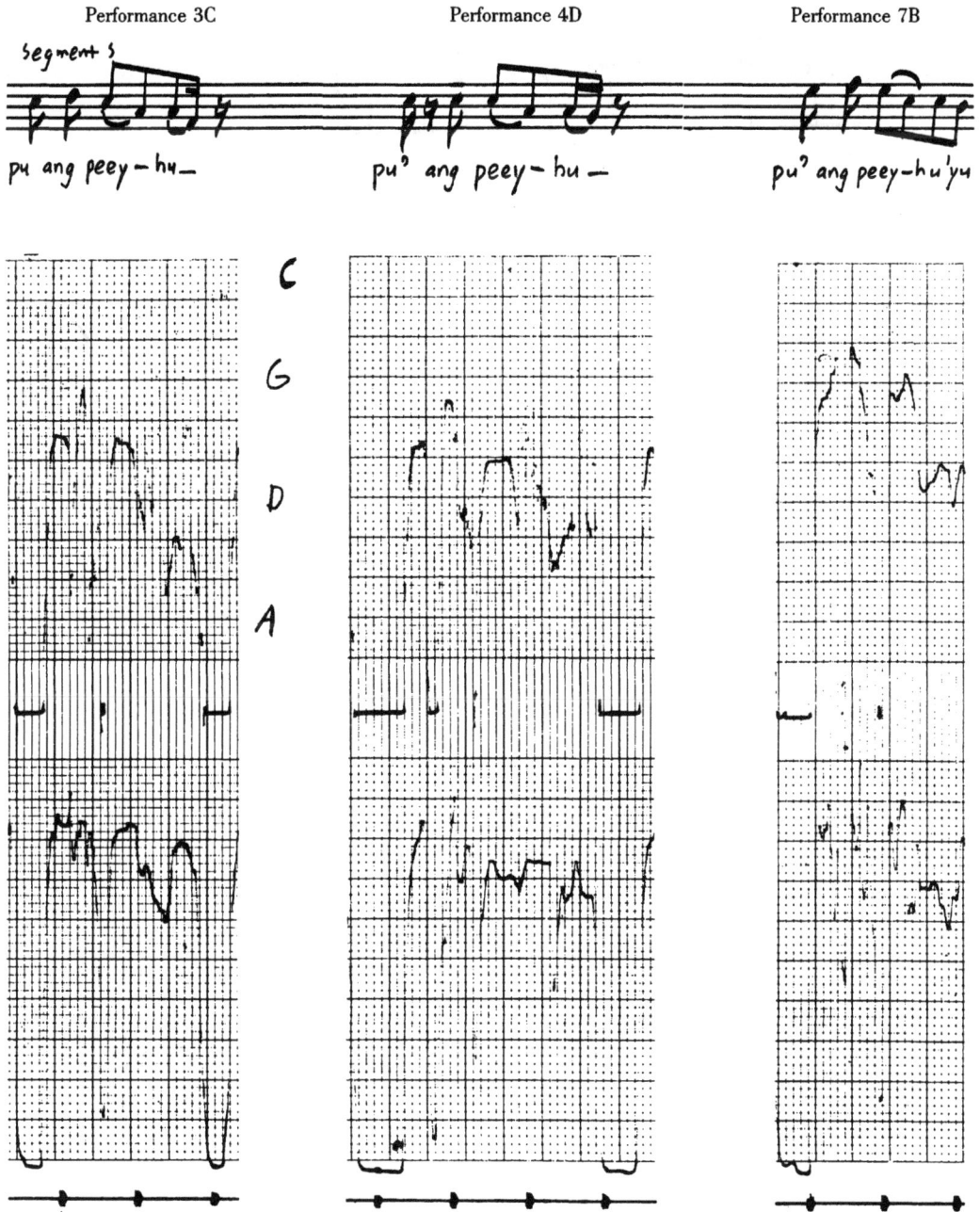

Figure 12. Occurrence of Breath Accent on Different Pitch Level than Syllable Extended

Chapter 3.
The Kachina Dance Song

3.1. The Kachina Dances

The kachina dances are performed by the members of the men's secret societies, each of which possesses a kiva, an underground ceremonial chamber. There were 11 such kivas in the First Mesa area at the time I carried on my field work. All adult male Hopi are members of the kachina cult, so all participate in the dances.

Beginning with the Powamu Ceremony in December, each men's secret society performs a kachina dance in its kiva for four consecutive weekends, a different one on each weekend. In almost all dances one only kachina is represented, as for example, the *Ma kachina* (the hunter), the *Heyheya kachina* (the farmer), or the *Angak*ᵛ*china* (the longhaired). Except for minor details, the masks and costumes of the men participating are similar, representing the particular kachina dancing. As they dance they sing through their masks, gesture with their free hand, and in most cases provide their own rhythmic accompaniment with idiophones, gourd rattles held in the hand and turtleshell rattles or sheep bells tied to their legs. In some dances an individual Hopi who does not dance will provide an accompaniment on a drum, or a group of *manas* (kachina maidens) will accompany the dancers with rasps placed against gourd resonators.

The dancing is ceremonial and restrained. A group of eight or more kachinas forms a file and dances in slow shuffling steps, making occasional about-faces. At some dances there is also a parallel file of a smaller number of *manas*. The *manas* are impersonated by younger men and their heads are decorated with the traditional "butterfly" hairdo of the unmarried Hopi woman, whorls extending from the sides of the head like wings. The participation of *manas* is apparently optional except in the case of the *Niman*, or Home Dance, the final dance of the summer, in which they always appear.

One of the men in the file of kachinas is the leader and initiates the dance by a sustained shake of his gourd rattle. I was told by an informant that the side dancer, uncle, or priest exhorts the dancers and interprets the text of the song with his gestures. The gestures of the kachinas also symbolize the key

words in the song but many of them are meaningless to the uninitiated (Kealiinohomoku 1967:343-45).

The dance routine performed by each type of kachina is differentiated by certain stylistic characteristics, as are the songs they sing. Within this framework there is considerable creativity and variation. Each time the kachinas dance in their kiva their song is to some extent different in both text and melody and there will be some variation in the dance steps, in the gestures made, and in the accompaniment provided by the idiophones. The turtleshell rattle or sheep bells tied to the leg will, of course, be heard every time that leg is advanced. The gourd rattle held in the right hand of the dancer is usually shaken with each footfall but there are occasional one-beat pauses. There are also hemiolas (three shakes of the rattle performed in the same space of time as two footfalls) and sustained shakes.

The dances in the kivas are witnessed by most of the Hopi of the village who are not participating, groups of spectators going from one kiva to another. In the summer some of these dances are repeated in the plazas. Most of these repetitions have been requested by a woman or a group of women who had witnessed the dance in the kiva and who sponsor its performance in the plaza. Such sponsorship is both expensive and time-consuming since the woman or women involved must provide food and drink for the day for the dancing kachinas, and the food and other presents distributed by the kachinas to the audience. Traditionally, boys in the audience are given bows and arrows and the girls kachina dolls.

In the kiva a song and its accompanying dance are performed once. Then there is a period of rest before a second song and dance. This process continues throughout the two-day weekend. In the plaza the same song and dance are performed two to four times on different sides of the plaza before the kachinas retire for a rest period. A priest leads them from one side of the plaza to the other by strewing a trail of cornmeal. Occasionally he also dusts the kachinas with cornmeal. During rest periods kachina clowns, usually called "mudheads," enter the plaza and engage in various antics. They also have their own characteristic songs. In addition to providing humor, what the clowns do can be considered a negative form of education for the younger Hopi present. Their actions, such as maltreating an animal, illustrate what a Hopi should not do.

3.2. The Composition of the Kachina Dance Songs

During the two days of the kachina dances in the plaza, as many as 15 different songs may be performed. Each performance may last from five to ten minutes. The songs sung at the kachina dances are usually composed for the occasion by individual Hopi men. Some men have developed a reputation as composers and the members of the secret society may ask one or more of them to compose a song for a particular kachina dance. Alternatively, a man may compose a needed song and come forward with it. The secret society will tactfully refuse both commissioned and proffered songs which they do not find suitable. They also customarily make changes in songs they have accepted but do not find fully appropriate. Such changes made by the group are usually of the words only, not of the melody. If insufficient newly composed songs are available, a group of the men may get together and compose the necessary songs. On occasion, they may use an already existing song which has been in wide favor, although very few kachina dance songs remain in the repertory for more than a few years. The individual composer traditionally accepts the changes made by the members of the secret society who will perform the song and it is he who teaches the song to the group, who learns it by rote.

The kachina dance songs are cast in a five-part form: AABBA. In most cases the B part is shorter than the A. Part B is usually composed of a short section of new material which is then followed by a repetition of material from A. In other cases B may consist entirely of material from A, but always with some variation of text and/or melody. When a Hopi man sings a kachina dance song for his children he usually sings the A part only once. If you ask him to sing a kachina dance song for you, and he is willing to do so, this is as much of it as he will sing. This study concerns only the A section.

The composer of a kachina dance song has a given structure and some material at hand before he begins his work. The A part of the song is itself divided into two sections. Both end with vocables sung in the lower register of the voice. The second section of A begins at a higher tessitura than the first. The type of

kachina which will sing the song is identified by an opening formula which precedes the first section of the A part. This formula, which I term the Identificatory Introduction, consists of otherwise meaningless syllables sung to a particular pattern of pitch and rhythm. The B part of the five-part form begins with the sung syllables *hapi mey*, which are not meaningful in spoken Hopi, but which in song are an indication that the singer is about to sing something new. Both the A and B parts end with what is termed the "Moccasin," which is approximately the same length as the Identificatory Introduction and, like it, consists of vocables. The last two-syllable group of the Moccasin is repeated and forms, according to my informants, the Identificatory Close, also symbolizing the particular kachina being represented.

I do not find the Identificatory Close as well differentiated as the Identificatory Introduction. The longhaired kachina is a very popular type and its Identificatory Introduction is therefore well known. In 1960 I played, for some of the older men at the First Mesa, the Identificatory Introductions of kachina dance songs recorded at Third Mesa in 1903 though 1905. They were able to identify only two of the Identificatory Introductions, both being of the Anga, or longhaired kachina. The Identificatory Introductions used at the First Mesa are so well known to the older Hopi that if one were to state that he would sing a particular kind of kachina dance song he might omit the Identificatory Introduction and begin instead with the first meaningful utterance of the song. Since he had already informed you of the type of kachina dance song he was about to sing, there would be no need to include the Identificatory Introduction. This is the case with several of the performances transcribed. (For further information concerning the composition of kachina dance songs, see List 1968.)

3.3. The Barefoot Long-Haired Kachina

There are two types of longhaired kachinas and they are usually differentiated by the Hopi as the one who wears moccasins and the one who goes barefoot. The longhaired kachina who wears moccasins is known as the *Angak·china* (ang-ak-china or an-gaqtsina) and the one who goes barefoot is known as *Katoch-Ang-ak·china*. The costume of the two types of longhaired kachina is quite similar, differing only in the color of body paint, the type of sash worn, carrying a spring of Douglas fir with the gourd rattle or wearing Douglas fir anklets, and going barefoot or wearing moccasins.

This chapter is concerned with the song of the *Katoch-Ang-ak'china*, the barefoot longhaired kachina, so I shall describe his costume. As its name indicates, this kachina wears long hair. The lower part of the mask covering the upper part of the face is covered by feathers. Above the beard there is a black line with rectangular panels of all colors. The kachina wears a ruff made of Douglas fir and carries a sprig of it in the right hand, which also holds the gourd rattle. Like most kachinas he wears a white, hand-woven cotton kilt with embroidered ends. This is secured with a white cotton braided wedding sash. A fox skin is suspended from the sash and hangs behind the dancer. The bare body above the kilt is painted pink (Colton 1949:49). He has a turtleshell tied to the back of his right leg below the knee. To this are attached sheep hooves which strike the shell as the leg is moved (Earle and Kennard 1938:9-10).

The provenance of the eight recordings of the *Katoch-Ang-ak'china tawi*, the barefoot longhaired kachina song, from which the transcriptions presented later are developed, is given in Figure 13 below, in chronological order. The arabic numbers represent the performances and the capital letters the singers. Singers B and C were twice recorded singing the song on different days. The performance by E is incomplete. Singers A-E were recorded singing the A part of the song only. The recording of singer F is of the entire song but only A part has been transcribed.

3.4. Corpus of Recordings to be Studied

Fewkes described Kakapti as an older Hopi priest (Folkways Record #FW 4394 liner notes). Singers B, C, and E were in their late 50s or early 60s at the time of recording, singer E in his late 70s. The first three had sufficient English to answer my questions without the help of others. My questions of E were often translated for him by his wife.

I was told by several of the Hopi men that singer D was a "poor singer." It was for this reason that I recorded him. It was my hope that the comparison of his performance with those of the others would assist in establishing the parameters of what was acceptable and what was not.

Singer F was in his early 40s at the time he recorded the song. He was disabled and made use of a wheelchair, and had not been active in Hopi traditional life for 20 years. He stated that he had learned the song from his grandmother. He had no knowledge of how or where she had learned it but he thought it was a very old song.

3.5. The Spoken Texts and Translations

In Figure 14 two versions are offered of the meaningful text of the barefoot kachina dance song and its translation into English. Both represent the text as it would be spoken, not as sung, so the vocables and

Figure 13. Provenance of the Kachina Dance Song Performances Transcribed

1A   Sung by Kakapti of the Village of Walpi, First Mesa. Recorded at Grand Canyon, Arizona, by J. Walter Fewkes, 2 June 1924. (According to a notation in a Gennet Records ledger, the recording was made in 1926 by a Mr. Harvey.) Issued by Gennett Records, #5757A; re-released as Folkways Records #FE 4394.

2B   Sung by a man from the village of Sichomovi, First Mesa. Recorded by George List at Polacca, Arizona, 1 August 1960.

3C   Sung by a man from the village of Sichomovi, First Mesa. Recorded by George List at Polacca, Arizona, 1 August 1960.

4D   Sung by a man from the village of Sichomovi, First Mesa. Recorded by George List at Polacca, Arizona, 1 August 1960.

5E   Sung by a man from the village of Sichomovi, First Mesa. Recorded by George List at Polacca, Arizona, 8 August 1960.

6C   Singer C, recorded by George List at Polacca, Arizona, 9 August 1960.

7B   Singer B, recorded by George List at Polacca, Arizona, 11 August 1960.

8F   Sung by a man of the Village of Hotevilla, Third Mesa. Self-recorded at Flagstaff, Arizona, August 1984.

(Since I did not receive permission from singers B-F to publish their names, I have omitted them. Singer A had, of course, already been identified on a commercial recording.)

breath accents heard in the sung versions are not reproduced. The two spoken versions are placed one above the other and are identified as I and III, the former representing the songs recorded at First Mesa, and the latter the one song recorded at Third Mesa. The English translation is placed between these two versions and unless otherwise indicated applies to both textual versions.

The spoken versions are segmented to correlate with the sung performances (Figure 15). Thus the letters A through Z placed above textual version I identify the segments and apply also to the segmentation of the English translation and to III found below. If the segment begins with lexically meaningful text, the segment letter will appear immediately above the first Hopi letter or free form of the segment. If a vocable occurs at that point in the sung performances, the space below the letter will necessarily be blank. If further blank spaces are found in the segment this indicates that further vocables are sung in this segment.

On occasion a Hopi word or free form will extend across segment boundaries. To indicate this the last letter of that part of the word or free form found at the end of a segment will be underlined and the line carried forward until it underlines the first letter of the segment in which the word or free form ends. An example of this is given below.

$$\begin{array}{ccc} & J & K \\ \text{taa} & \text{wa} & \text{nawita} \end{array}$$

(*Taawanawita* is thus one word or free form which spans three segments.)

The translation into English is usually word by word, but occasionally may represent a group of words. Alternative readings are given in parentheses, as are indications of number. Thus (DU) signifies "dual," that is, two persons or objects are involved rather than one or more than two. (NSG) indicates "non-singular," more than one object or person, either dual or plural, two or more than two. (PL) means more than two objects or persons.

At a few points textual version III differs from textual version I. In these cases a separate English translation is given. Otherwise the translation offered for I also applies to III.

Figure 14. Transcription and Translation of the Spoken Text

	A		B		C
I	iyaaha	imöyhoyatu	iyaaha	imömu	umuhkway
	Honored	my (DU) little grandchildren.	Honored	my (PL) grandchildren,	your grandfather
III	haw uma	imöyhoyatu	haw uma	imömu	umuukway
	hey, you!		hey, you!		
		D		E	
I	uuyiyat	ang	yookva	ang	paatalawva
	his plants, (i.e., cornfield)	on them	it rained.	There	it got to be shiny with water.
III	uuyiyat	ang	yokva	ang	paatalawva
	F		G		H
I	aw	uma	munlalay____toni		imömu
	There (to)	you (NSG)	go channel pools of	water to other plants	my (PL) grand-children
III	aw	uma	munlalay____toni		taawa____nawita
					Through-out the day
	I				J K
I	umuhkway	uma	amum	momortoni	taa____wa____nawita
	Your grand-father	you (NSG)	with him	go to swim.	Through-out the day
III	umuukway	uma	amum	momortoni	
		L	M		N
I	liiẙa		itahso	itahkway	uuyiyat	itamuy
	right here.		Our (NSG) grandmother,	our, (NSG) grandfather	(To) his plants (i.e., cornfield)	we (NSG)
III			itaaso	itaakway	uuyiyat	itamuy
			O		P	
I	aw	ökiqw'ö	itahkway	uuyico'at	kuwan'ewsoniwa
	there to	when arriving (PL)	our grand-father	his plants (i.e., corn)	pretty colors appear.
III	aw	pituqw'ö when arriving (DU)	itaakway	uuyi'at	kuwan'ewsoniwa

Figure 14. *(Continued)*

Q

I	itamu	ang	uysonaq	waymakyangw	taymaqw
	We	along	through the corn plants,	while walking along,	while looking around
III	itamuy	ang	uysonaq	waymakyangw	taymaqw

R   **S**

I	sipepetota	pu'	ang	peehu	
	lots of flowers (i.e., tassels),	(and) then	there	some	
	silpepetota	pu'	ang	peehu	pay already

T   **U**

I	sivöwiwyungma	kaway'uyi'at	melon'uyi'at
	they are flowerless and now forming corn.	His watermelon plants,	his muskmelon plants,
III	sivöwiwyungwa	kaway'uyi'at	melon'uyi'at

V

I	pölöneyang	hotam'iwta	ahaw
	mixed in round (i.e., little melon balls in them)	stretched out (i.e. have runners).	Say,
III	pölöneyang	hotam'iwta	ahhaw

W   **X**   **Y**

I	itupko	owi	oovi	itam	hahlayi	itahso'
	my younger brother	Yes.	Consequently, therefore,	we (NSG)	happy.	Our (NSG) grandmother.
III	itupko	owi	oovi	itam	haalayi	itahso'

Z

I	is haw	is uni	askwali
	Wow!	How nice!	Thank you (female speaking).
III	is haw	is uni	askwali

Notes

1. A guide to the pronunciation of Hopi will found in the appendix. (See also 2.2.6, p. 00.)

2. The first free form in segments A and B of textual version I, *iyaaha*, was translated by my second Hopi translator as "honored" or "honorable." He said the word was never used in common speech but was heard fairly often in song. The word is not found in Seaman's *Hopi Dictionary* and Malotki's Hopi informant at Third Mesa did not know the word. Malotki therefore believed *iyaaha* to be vocables. However, the Third Mesa singer, F, employs meaningful utterances at the beginnings of segments A and B and I assume the First Mesa singers would do the same. I therefore have represented this combination of phones as a meaningful utterance, as indicated by my second translator. My assumption is that *iyaaha* is an archaic word. Archaic words are often heard in song, particularly in songs of a religious or mythological character (Fewkes in Frisbie 1977:12).

3. According to Malotki, *haw*, found at the beginnings of segments A and B in textual version III, is an expletive used to gain attention. I have translated it as "hey." Other colloquial expressions also have been used in translating the Hopi into English when it seemed appropriate.

4. In segment K of version I appears the word *liiƚa*, translated as "right here," which my second Hopi translator said was a Zuni word commonly used in Hopi song. The barred l, the voiceless l (ƚ), is employed in Zuni but not in Hopi. Words from other Indian languages, particularly Zuni, are commonly employed in Hopi kachina dance songs (List 1968:51). Of the singers of the First Mesa only A sang *liiƚa* in segment K. The others whom I recorded at First Mesa in 1960, B-E, sang vocables at this place which did not include the ƚ. Whether *liiƚa* is an instance of vocables or a meaningful utterance is difficult to determine. I have selected the second alternative here. It should be noted that singer A followed *liiƚa* with a vocable containing a ƚ. Malotki's informant, singer F, was of the opinion that this section of the song consisted of Zuni vocables.

5. In version I, segment N, the third free form is *ökiqw'ö*, while in III it is *pituqw'ö*. The first represents the plural, the second the dual form of the verb translated as "when arriving." In the dual form only two individuals are arriving, in the plural more than two.

6. The particle, *pay*, found in segment S of III, but not in I, is translated as "already." In this translation *pay* has been interpreted as representing the temporal mode. It can also represent the assertive mode. In the latter case the two free forms *ehu pay* would appropriately be translated as "quite a few." However, its temporal form seems the most appropriate here.

7. The first free form in segment V of III, *ahhaw*, was given by Malotki as two free forms, *ah haw*. I have combined them for ease in comparison with spoken version I. According to Malotki, this is not a Third Mesa word, but represents a type of exclamation. It has been translated as "say!"

3.6. Comparison of the Two Spoken Versions of the Text

3.6.1. Comparison of Words or Free Forms

In most cases the same words or free forms are seen in versions I and III, and in the same order. To this there are a few exceptions, some of which have been partially noted above. These exceptions are listed below and are grouped under the headings: substitution, transposition, and omission/addition. The first two terms, I believe, are self-explanatory. The term "omission/addition" is used when a word appears in one spoken version but not in the other. In using these terms I am not necessarily implying that one spoken version antedates the other.

3.6.1a. Substitution

In version I the first free form in segments A and B is *iyaaha*, which is translated as "honored." In version III two free forms are found in this place instead, *haw uma*, translated as "hey, you!" In segment K of version I there is found the free form *liiƚa*. In all other performances vocables are sung instead. In version I the third free form of segment N is *ökiqwˀö*, while in version III it is *pituqwˀö*.

3.6.1b. Transposition

The free form *taawanawita*, translated as "throughout the day," is seen in a different place in version I than in version III. In version I it begins as the last portion of segment I, continues through segment J, and concludes with the first portion of segment K. In version III this free form begins in the second portion of segment G and is completed in segment H.

3.6.1c. Omission/Addition

The free form *imömu*, translated as "my grandchildren," occurs in version I at the beginning of segment H. It does not appear in version III. This free form is seen previously in both versions in segment B, but not in version III in that section of the song comprising segments F-K. On the other hand, the free form *pay*, translated as "already," which appears in version III as the fourth free form of segment S, is not seen in version I.

3.6.2. Comparison of Phones

In subsequent discussion I shall indicate segment, position of the free form within the segment, and the location of the letters within the free form in abbreviated fashion. The three elements will be separated by periods. Thus F.2.4 represents segment F, the second free form of the segment, and the fourth letter or phone within that free form. If more than one letter or phone is involved a hyphen will be employed. Thus .4-5 refers to both the fourth and fifth letters of the free form, and .4-6 to the fourth, fifth, and sixth letters or phones of the free form.

No transpositions of letters or phones are found in either the spoken versions of the song or in its sung performances. In dealing with phones or groups of phones the term "elision" seems more appropriate than omission. I shall therefore employ the term "elision/addition" rather than "omission/addition." This terms applies when a phone or phones appears in one spoken version and not in the other. For example, in version I a prefix is written as *si* while in version III it is written *sil*. This is indicated as .0/3. The zero indicates that this phone does not appear in this particular free form in version I but does occur as the third letter in the free form in version III. (The reader should observe that the slash will be employed with a different meaning, that of a ratio, in contour analysis. Here it represents an alternative reading.) The glottal stop is counted as a letter.

In the analysis of the song text, categorization will be based upon what is written and not necessarily upon what is heard. Thus *u* vs. *uu* will be considered an elision/addition as will be *u* vs. *uy*. A long vowel may differ phonetically from a short vowel and it may be said that when a glide is attached to a vowel the resultant diphthong differs phonetically from its two constituent vowels when they are produced independently, one following another.

Below I list those disparities between the two spoken versions of the text which apparently do not affect meaning. These probably reflect dialect differences between Hopi speech at the First Mesa and the Third Mesa areas. Conversely, they may be due to different conceptualizations of what is heard by the linguists in transcribing or, in some cases, faults in articulation by those who spoke or sang the Hopi.

3.6.2a. Substitution

The most common example of this phenomenon is the use of *ah* in version I where *aa* is employed in version III. This is particularly evident in that part of a free form representing the possessive, "our," *itah* vs. *itaa*. This can be seen in M.1.3-4, M.2.3-4, O.1.3-4, and Y.1.3-4. This substitution also occurs in the free form meaning "happy," *hahlayi* vs. *haalayi*, X.3.2-3. A similar type of substitution, but involving a different vowel, occurs in the possessive "your," *umuh* vs. *umuu*, C.1.3-4 and I.1.3-4. In the above example the vowel is aspirated rather than lengthened or vice versa. There is, in addition, one case in which there is a substitution of consonants, *m* vs. *w*, in T.1.12. This is in a rather long free form, *sivöwiwyuhgma* vs. *sivöwiwyuhgwa*.

3.6.2b. Elision/Addition

In R.1.0/3 version III has an *l* which is absent in version I. Contrasting the full free forms it is *sipepetota* vs. *silpepetota*, meaning "lots of flowers." In V.1.0/2, version III has an *h* and this letter is absent in version I, *ahaw* vs. *ahhaw*; the form is translated as the expletive, "say!"

3.6.2c. Substitution or Elision/Addition

As indicated above, the next two cases could be considered to fall under the heading substitution rather than elision/addition, but are included under the latter heading for the reasons given. In D.2.0/3 a short vowel is contrasted with a long vowel, *yokva* vs. *yookva*. The meaning is "it rained." In the second case, Q.1.0/6, the glide *y* follows the vowel in version III but not in I. The two forms are *itamu* vs. *itamuy*, signifying "we."

3.7. The Sung Peformances

Figure 15 is a comparative score, since what is found in the nine staves is *not* performed simultaneously. Rather, these are discrete performances which have been placed one above the other for purposes of comparison. The fact that Figure 15 is a comparative score is indicated by the lack of a connecting brace, bracket, or vertical line at the left of the score.

The transcriptions are in pitch band notation and therefore carry no clef sign. However, the lines and spaces represent those of the bass clef (see 2.1.2, p. 00). The kachina dance songs have a fairly regular pulse but are not metrical. In tempo they range from MM 108 through MM 156 to an eighth note, the former representing the performance by singer F and the latter that of singer C. Since there is no meter, all notes sung to one word or free form are beamed together when possible. It is not possible, of course,

if part of the segment must be represented by the value of a quarter note or longer.

Performance 5E is incomplete. After singing segments A-C the singer erroneously sang segment P instead of D and then part of Q. His wife immediately stopped him, informing him that he was not singing the song correctly. The singer refused to try again. His partial performance is included along with the rest, however.

As can be seen in the chronological listing of recordings given in Figure 13, two singers, B and C, were recorded on two different days. The performances by each are placed one above the other rather than in chronological order for purposes of comparison. The Hopi men with whom I worked were of the opinion that the performances by singer C were closer in style to that of singer A (recorded many years earlier), than those of the other singers recorded from the First Mesa. Performances 3C and 6C are therefore placed immediately below 1A so that the comparison needed to check this statement can be more easily accomplished.

In singer B's first performance, 2B, he repeated the first section of the song, segments A-L. His first singing of this section is marked 2Ba and its repetition is marked 2Bb. Singer F did the same. Thus his first singing of the section is marked 8Fa and its repetition 8Fb. This singer also repeats segment Z and the moccasin, indicated as 8Fc.

Singers B and E do not begin with the Identificatory Introduction. (For an explanation of this omission, see 3.2, p. 00.) Of the ten staves found in the first page of the score, five are empty, 2Ba, 7B, and 5E because the Identificatory Introduction has been omitted, 2Bb and 8Fb because the Identificatory Introduction is not sung when the first section of the song is repeated. In all performances but one the moccasin contains four groups of vocables. The exception is found in 4D, where the singer extends the moccasin to seven groups.

In some cases the singer omits a segment or parts of a segment. When meaningful words are omitted the musical staff is left blank. The words not sung are given within brackets so that the reader will understand what the singer omitted.

In Figure 15 all vocables have been underlined. Additions to the meaningful words in singing have only been underlined when they form a syllable, that is, when they consist of or contain a vowel.

The syllables of the Hopi words are divided by hyphens. When the word extends from one segment to another, the crossing of the segment boundaries is indicated by two or more hyphens.

Figure 15. Comparative Score of Performances of the Kachina Dance Song

Figure 15. *(Continued)*

Figure 15. *(Continued)*

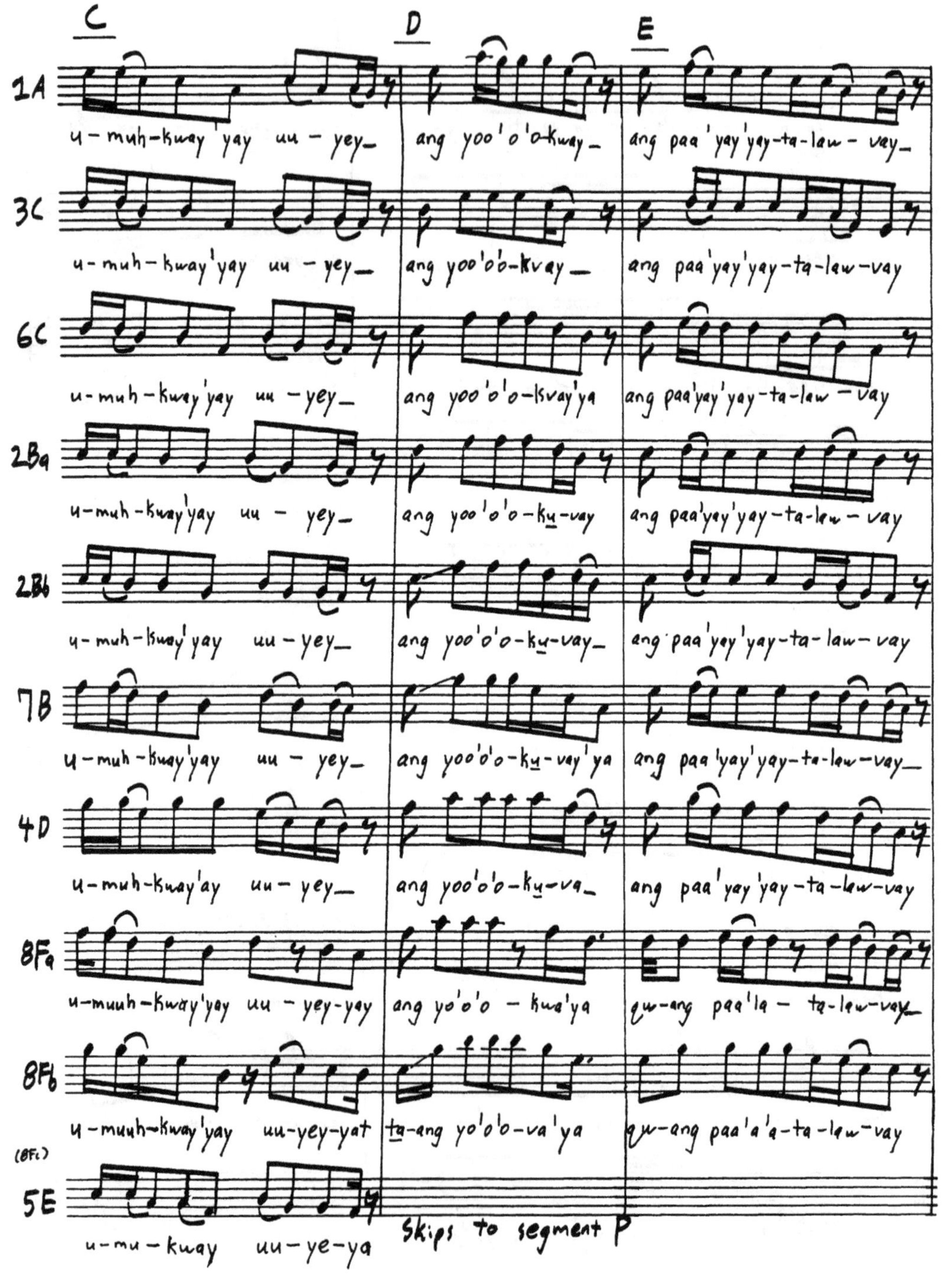

Figure 15. *(Continued)*

Figure 15. *(Continued)*

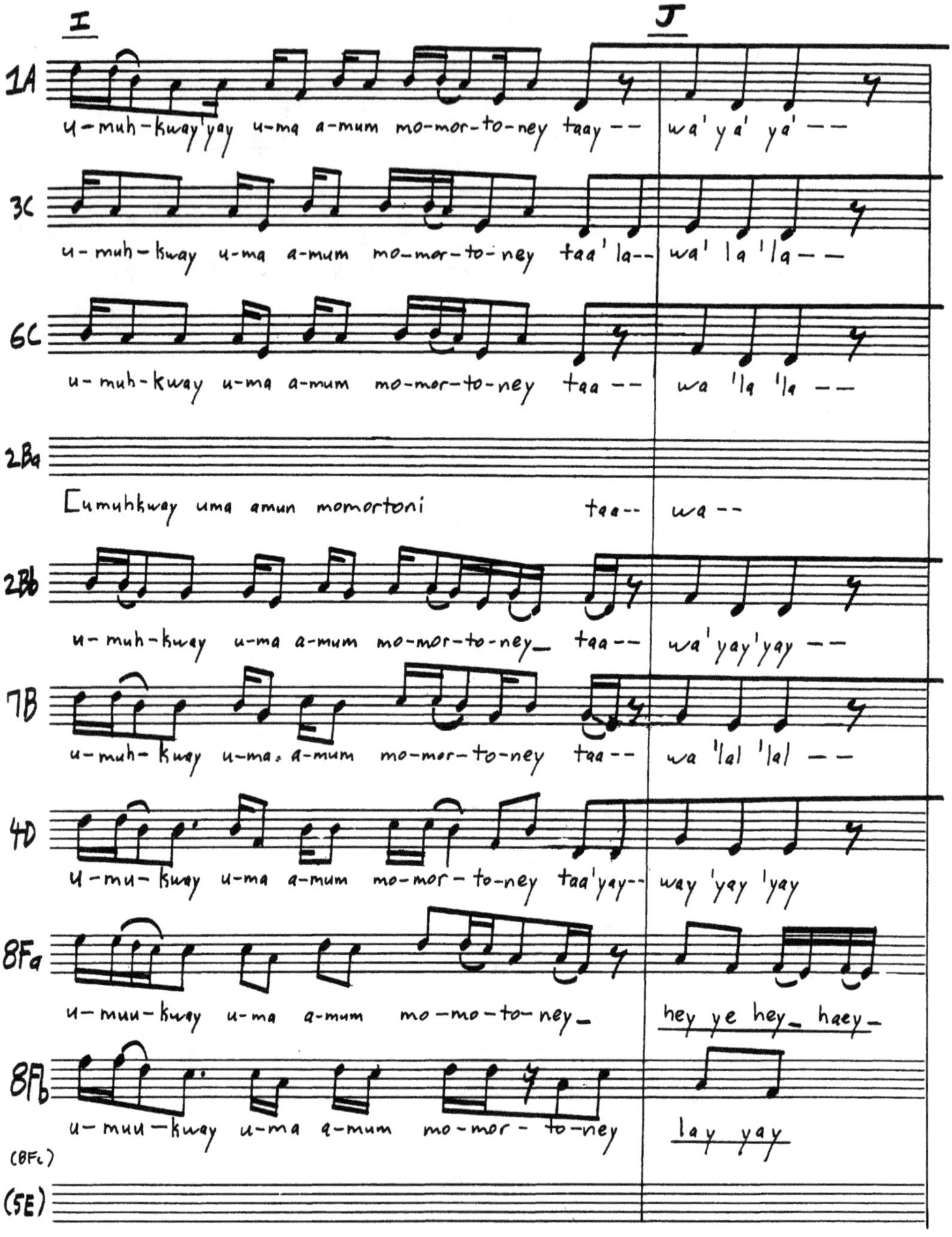

Figure 15. *(Continued)*

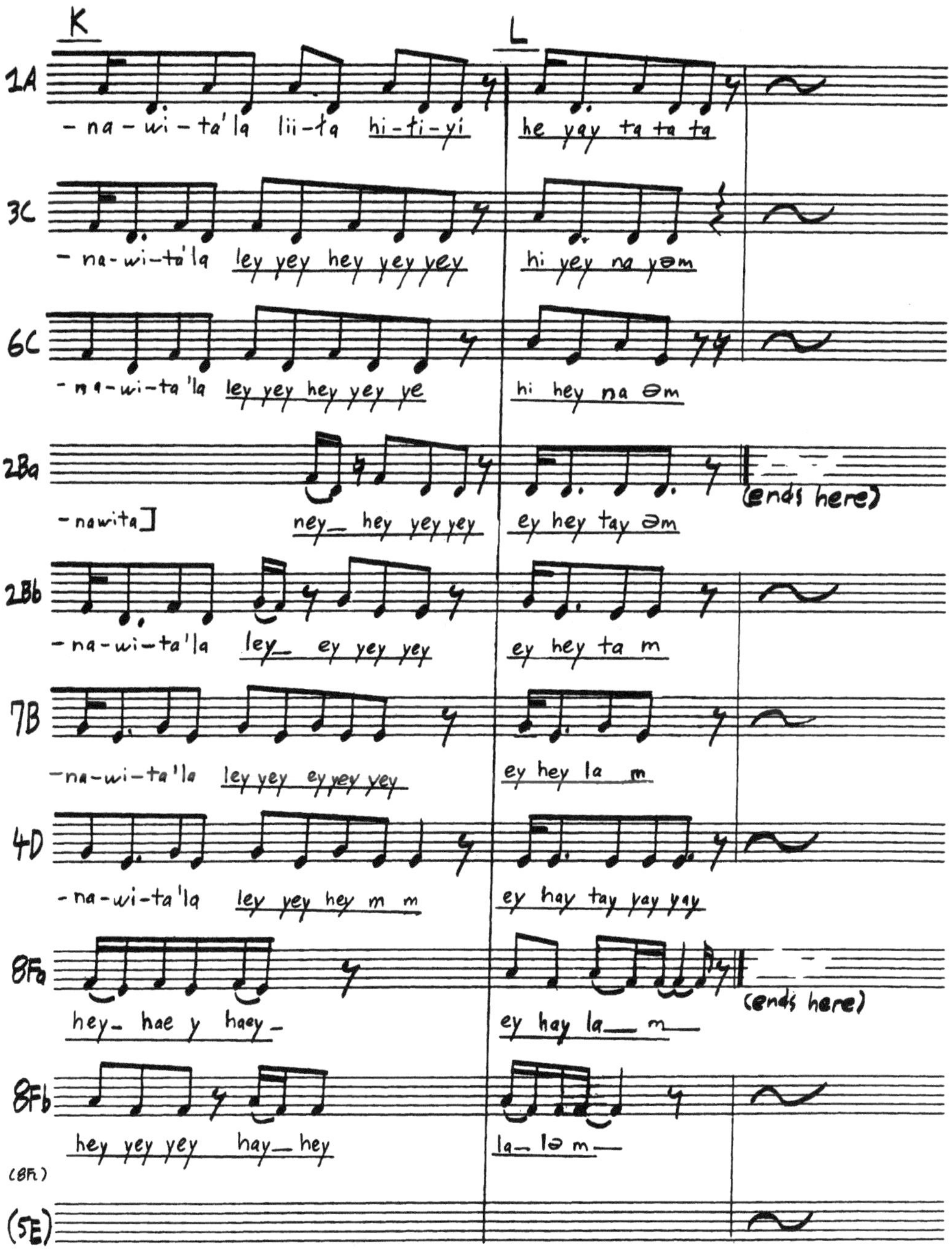

Figure 15. *(Continued)*

Figure 15. *(Continued)*

Figure 15. *(Continued)*

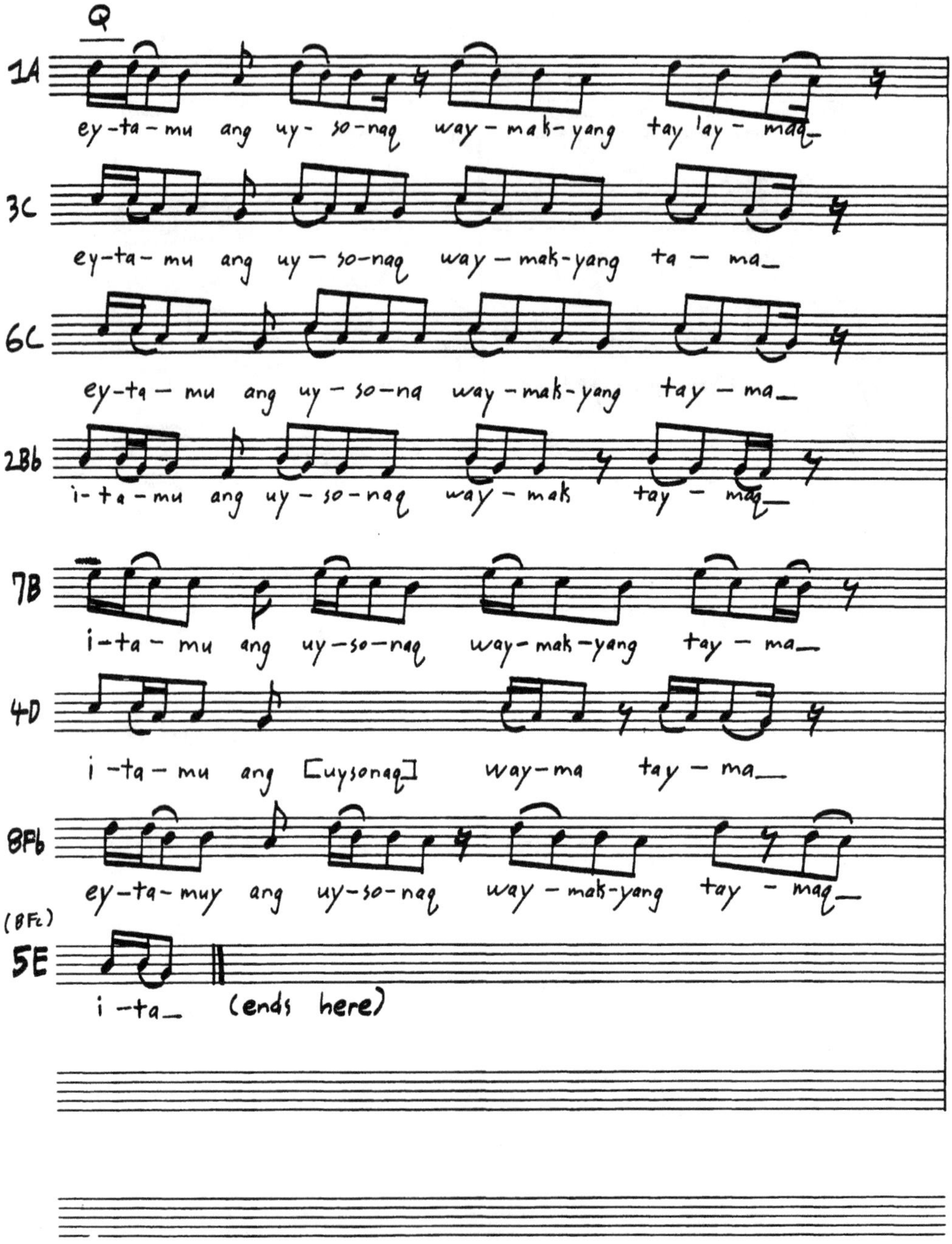

Figure 15. *(Continued)*

Figure 15. *(Continued)*

1A ka-way—u-i—at me-lon—u-i—at pö-lö—ne-ya ho-tam—iw—tay'yay

3C ka-way—u-i-at me-lon—u-i-at pö-lö-ne-ya ho-tam—in—tay'ley

6C ka-way-u-i-at me-lon—u-i-at pö-lö—ne-ya ho-tam—iw—tay'ley

2Bb ka-way—u-i-at me-lon—u-i pö-lö—ne-yang ho-tam—iw-tay'ley

7B ka-way-u-i-at me-lon-u-i pö-lö—ne-yang ho-tam—iw—tay'ay

4D ka-way-u-i-at me-lon-u-i pö-lö—ne-yang ho-tam—iw-tay'ay

8FB ka-way-u-i-at me-lon—u-i-at pö-lö-ne-yang ho-taw—iw-tay'yay

(8Fc)

Figure 15. *(Continued)*

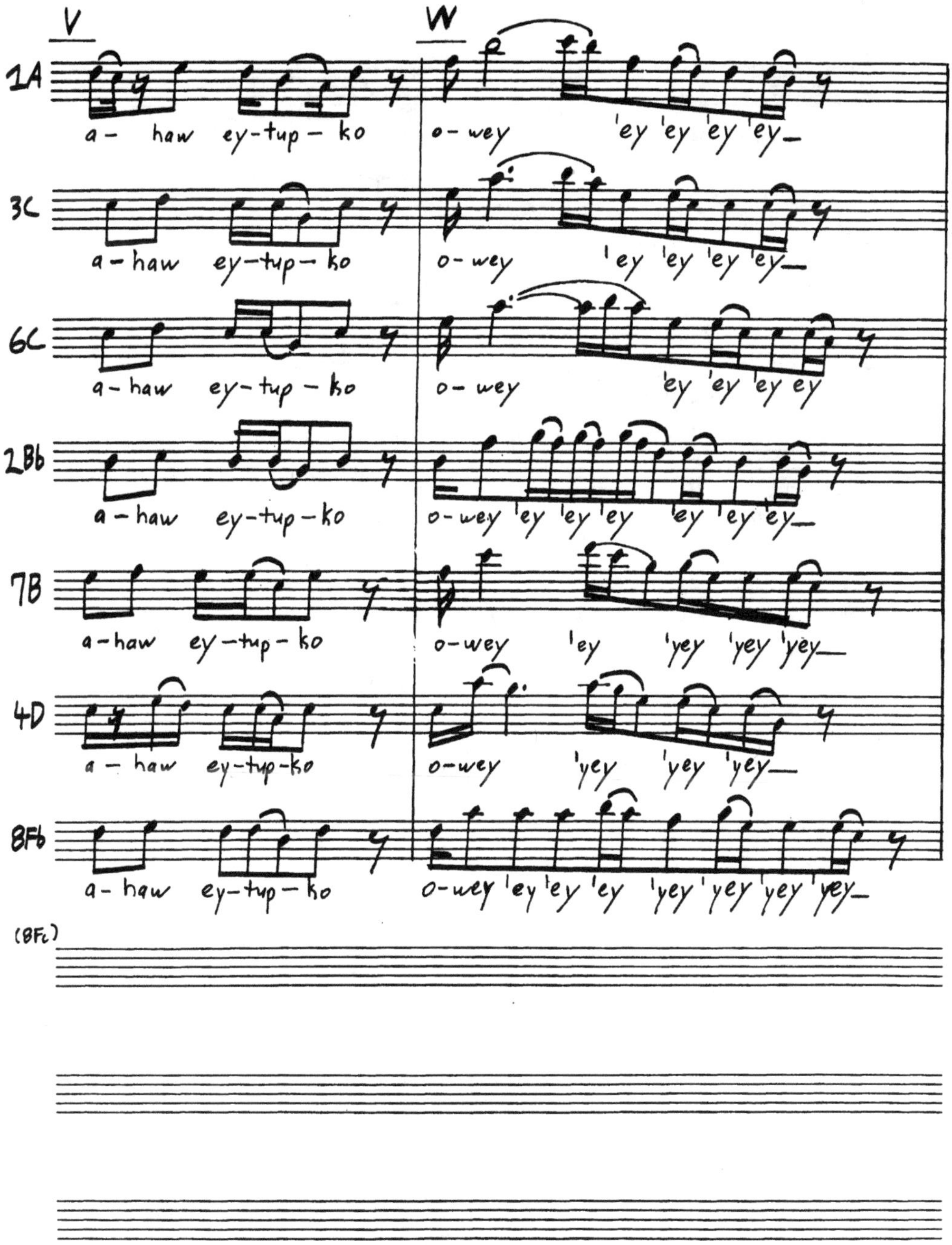

Figure 15. *(Continued)*

Figure 15. *(Continued)*

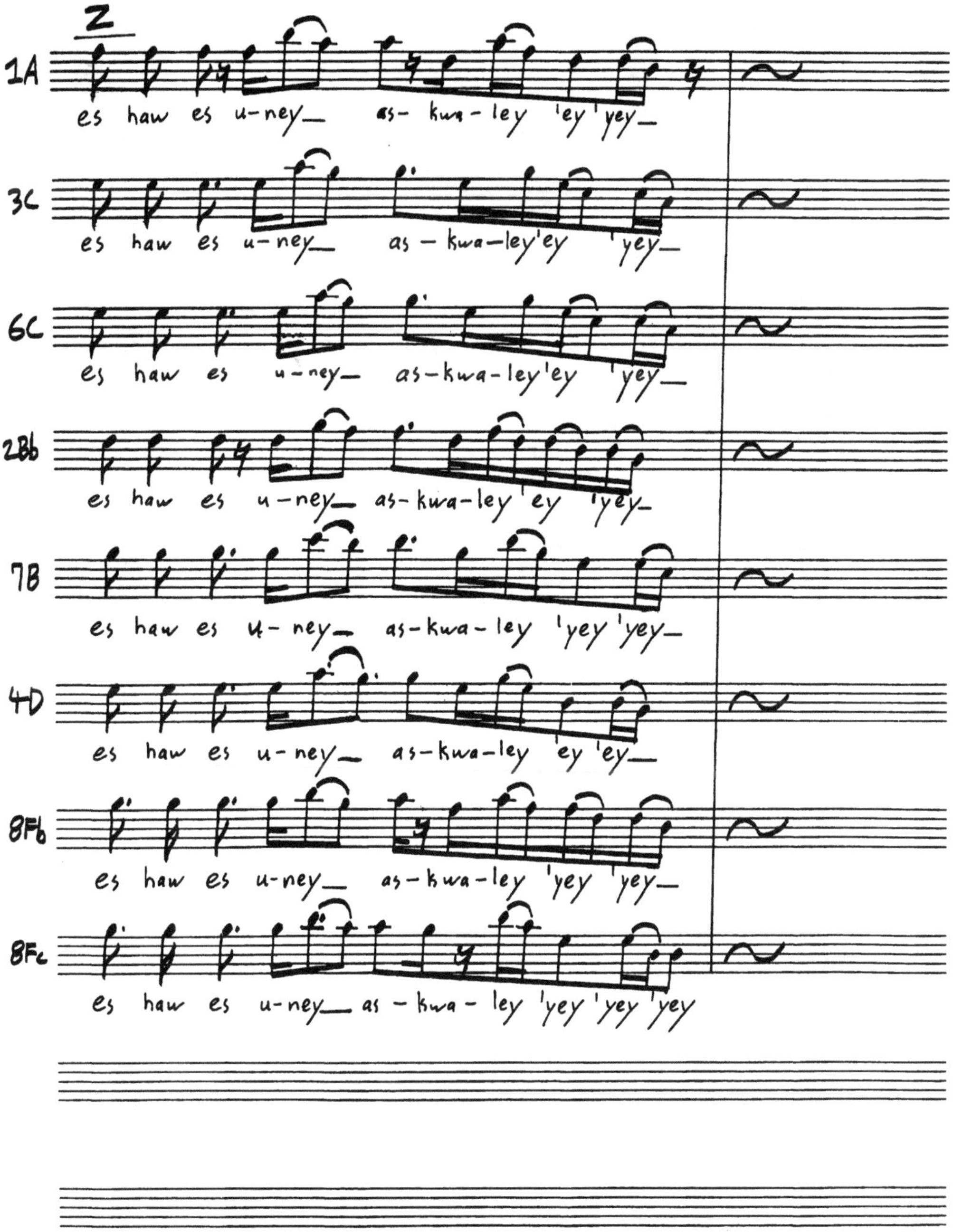

Figure 15. *(Continued)*

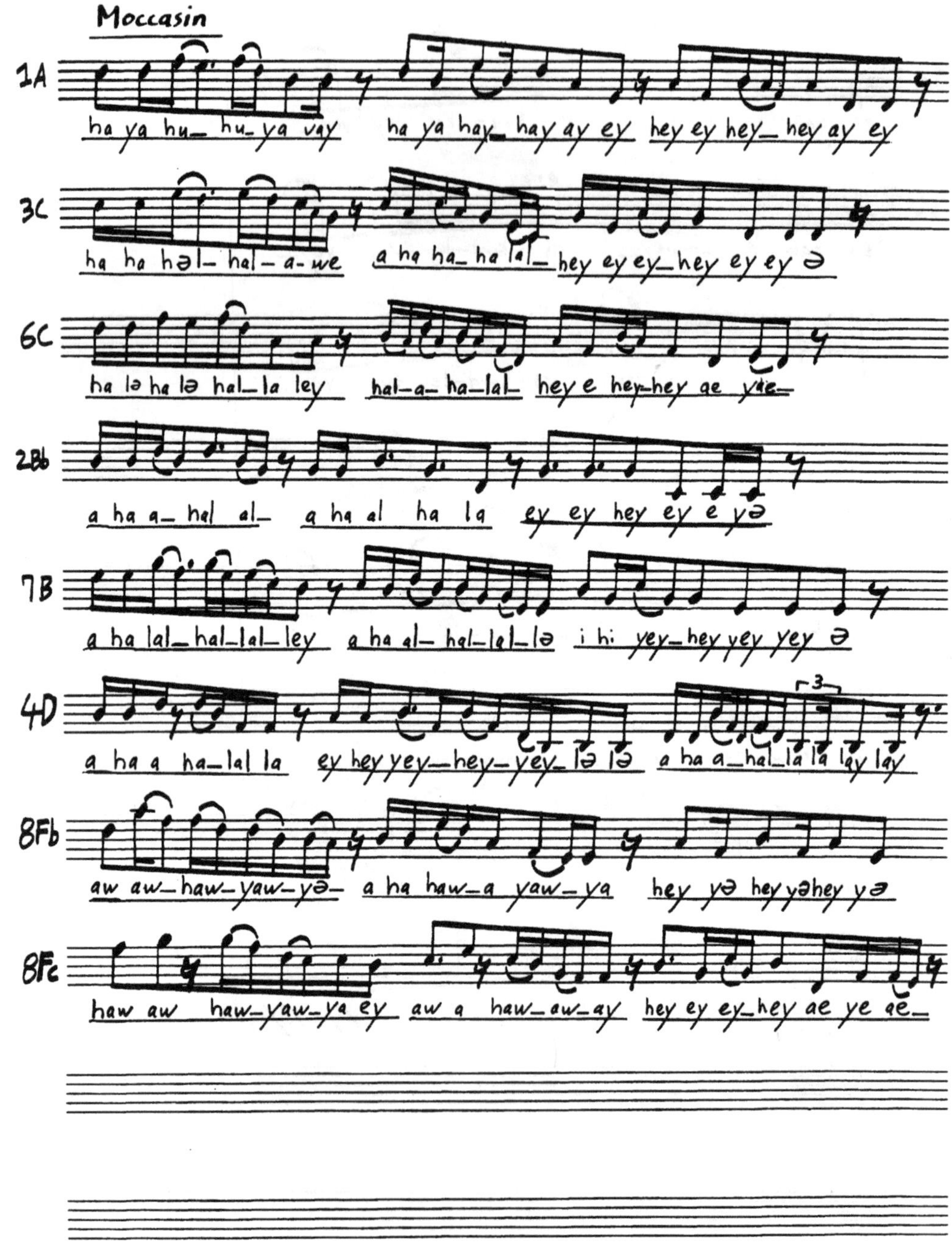

Figure 15. *(Continued)*

Notes

1. In performance 2Ba the singer omits segments I and J and the first portion of K, and then sings the vocables heard in the second portion of segment K and those heard in segment L. This may have been merely an error, but I have reason to believe that at this point the singer became dissatisfied with his performance, tacked on the usual ending of vocables, and then returned to repeat this section of part A, hoping to improve his performance.

2. Singer D was said to be a poor singer (see 3.4). It should be noted that in his performance of the song he omits a free form in both segments O and Q.

3. Since the pitch band is a whole tone in width (see 2.1.2), gradual raising or lowering of the pitch level which does not exceed this interval is not represented. For example, in performance 4D, beginning with segment Q, the singer gradually raises his pitch level until at segment V he is singing a semitone higher, the pattern being F descending to D^b and then to C, rather than E descending to C and then to B. At segment W he begins to lower the pitch level and by segment Y has lowered by a quarter tone.

4. The breath accent has been defined as the extension of a meaningful syllable. Vocables are also extended in the same manner, that is, by a rhythmic movement of the diaphragm. However, since these are not meaningful syllables, extensions are indicated only by repeated notes. In such cases no apostrophe precedes the repetition or modified repetition of the vowel or syllable.

5. In the vocables bilabials such as *m* are considered vowels since they can be sustained.

6. There are several places where it was not clear whether single syllables represented a separate word or free form or that two such adjacent syllables, as in segment Z, *is haw*, should be grouped together to form a single word or free form. Since at times two such adjacent syllables are translated with one English word, they have been considered one free form in the later comparison of the sung and spoken texts (Fig. 34). Here they are separated only by a single space to indicate the possibility that they might be considered as two separate entities.

7. In some cases there is a rhythmic pulsation, each an eighth note in value on sustained pitches. Such pulsations can be clearly heard but are not sufficiently pronounced to be written out as breath accents. In such cases the pulsations heard within a sustained pitch are indicated by dots placed over the note. This phenomenon is seen in segment P.

I was told by the Hopi men with whom I discussed the matter that three modifications of the form of part A of a kachina dance song were common. These included the omission of the Identificatory Introduction, the repetition of the first section of part A, and the extension of the Moccasin. I divide these modifications into two types. The first type can only be made out of context; the second type can be made either in or out of context. The omission of the Identificatory Introduction obviously is of the first type. It cannot be omitted by the kachinas while dancing. The repetition of the first segment of the A part, that is, the repetition of segments A through L, and the extension of the moccasin are of the second type. If employed at a public kachina dance, the modification must have been introduced at rehearsal and agreed upon by the participants. If sung by an individual out of context, either modification can be made at will. The repetition by singer F of segment Z and the Moccasin obviously is of the second type. This last form of repetition was not mentioned to me by any of my informants at the First Mesa. It may be a Third Mesa tradition.

3.8. Analysis of the Music

3.8.1. Comparison of the Melodic Contours

Figure 16 offers a contour analysis of all segments of the eight performances of the barefoot longhaired kachina dance song. (For the methods employed in contour analysis, see 2.1.5). The contours of the four melodic groups of the moccasin are also given here but the analysis of the contours of the Identificatory Introduction will be deferred until later.

In Figure 16 the first column represents the performances. The subsequent columns give the contours for each segment, the letters of the segments analyzed appearing above the columns. For example, the contour sung in performance 1A in segment A is HLM and the contour sung in performance 6C in segment B is HL. The moccasin as sung by singer D contains seven groups. Only four such groups are found in the moccasin as sung by the other singers.

Figure 16. Contour Analysis of the Kachina Dance Song

	A	B	C	D	E
1A	H L M	H L	H L	M H L	M H L
3C	H L H	H L	H L	M H L	M H L
6C	H L H	H L	H L	M H L	M H L
2Ba	M H L	H L	H L	M H L	M H L
2Bb	H L H	H L	H L	M H L	M H L
7B	M L H	H L	H L	M H L	M H L
4D	H L H	H L	H L	M H L	M H L
8Fa	M H L M	H L	H L	M H L	M H L
8Fb	M H L M	M H L	H L	L H M	M H L
5E	H L H	H L	H L		

	F	G	H	I	J
1A	M H L	L H L	H L	H L	H L
3C	M H L	L H M	H L	H L	L H L
6C	M H L	L H M	H L	H L	H L
2Ba	M H L	H L H	H L		
2Bb	L H M	L H L·	H L	H L	H L
7B	M H L	L H M	H L ·	H L	H L
4D	L H L	L H L	H L	H L	L H M
8Fa	M H L	M H L	H L M	H L	H L
8Fb	M H L	M H L	H L	H L M	H L

	K	L	M	N	O
1A	H L	H L	M H L	M H L M	H L
3C	H L	H L	M H L	M H L M	H L
6C	H L	H L	M H L	M H L M	H L
2Ba	H L	R			
2Bb	M^2 L H M^1	H L	M H L	M H L M	H L M
7B	H L	H L	M H L	M H L M	H L M

Figure 16. *(Continued)*

	K	L	M	N	O
4D	H L	R	M H L	M H L M	H L
8Fa	H L	H L			
8Fb	H L	H L	M^2 H L M^1	M H L M	H L

	P	Q	R	S	T
1A	M^2 H L M^1	H L	H L H	M H L	H L H
3C	M^2 H L M^1	H L	H L H	M H L	H L H
6C	M^2 H L M^1	H L	H L H	M H L	H L H
2Bb	M^2 H L M^1	H L	H L H	M H L	H L H
7B	M^2 H L M^1	H L	H L H	M H L	H L H
4D	M^2 H L M^1	H L	H L H	H L	H L H
8Fb	M^2 H L M^1	H L	H L H	H L	H L H
5E	M^2 H L M^1	H L			

	U	V	W	X	Y
1A	H L H	M H L M	M H L	H L M	H L H
3C	H L H	M L H	M H L	H L M	H L H
6C	H L H	M L H	M H L	H L M	H L H
2Bb	H L H	M H L M	M H L	H L M	H L H
7B	H L H	M H L M	M H L	H L M	H L H
4D	H L H	M H L M	M H L	H L M	H L H
8FB	H L H	M H L M	M H L	H L M	H L H

	Z	Moc. 1	Moc. 2	Moc. 3	Moc. 4
1A	M H L	M H L	M H L	M H L	H L
3C	M H L	M H L	H L	M H L	H L
6C	M H L	M H L	M H L	M H L	H L
2Bb	M H L	M H L	M H L	M H L	H L
7B	M H L	M H L	M H L	M H L	H L
4D	M H L	M H L	M H L	M H L	H L
8Fb	M H L	M H L	M H L	M H L	M H L
8Fc	M H L	M H L	M H L	M H L	M H L

Notes

1. Singer D omits free forms in segments O and Q of performance 4D, with no effect upon the contours derived from these segments. The contours are the same as those sung by all the other singers.

In the contour analysis I have considered singer D's sixth and seventh groups to be cognate with the third and fourth groups in the performances by the other singers. The contours given for 4D in groups 3 and 4 of the moccasin therefore represent, in reality, the sixth and seventh segments. Consideration of singer D's groups 3, 4, and 5 have been omitted. Since some of the singers repeat part of the song, and others do not sing every segment, as many as ten and as few as seven contours may be given for a segment.

Figure 17 offers the results of the contour analysis in tabular form. The first column identifies the segment by letter name; the next column gives the contour most frequently sung in this segment. In the third column is the ratio of occurrence of this particular contour. Thus 6/7 signifies that this contour is sung to six out of seven performances of this segment. The fourth column gives the percentage of

occurrence of this contour as derived from the ratio in column three. In figuring percentages I drop all numbers except the first two following the decimal point. Thus .75932 becomes 75 percent.

In Figure 17 there is a 100 percent concurrence of the contours sung in almost half of the segments, 14 out of 30. In 25 of the 30 segments the most frequent contour occurs at least 75 percent of the time. Thus the cultural norm I have set is achieved in 83 percent of the segments. (See 2.4)

What of the remaining five segments? In three of these one contour pattern occurs 71 percent of the time, which is not very far from the norm set. The remaining two contours are found in segment A, 50 percent and segment G, 44 percent. Segment A is the first sung by several of the singers. In my work with the songs of other cultures I have found the beginning of a song is where error is most likely to

Figure 17. Results of the Contour Analysis of the Kachina Dance Song

SEGMENT	MOST FREQUENT CONTOUR	RATIO	PERCENTAGE
A	H L H	5/10	50%
B	H L	9/10	90
C	H L	10/10	100
D	M H L	8/9	88
E	M H L	9/9	100
F	M H L	7/9	77
G	L H L	4/9	44
H	H L	8/9	88
I	H L	7/8	87
J	H L	6/8	75
K	H L	8/9	88
L	H L	7/9	77
M	M H L	6/7	85
N	M H L M	7/7	100
O	H L	5/7	71
P	M^2 H L M^1	8/8	100
Q	H L	8/8	100
R	H L	7/7	100
S	M H L	5/7	71
T	H L H	7/7	100
U	H L H	7/7	100
V	M H L M	5/7	71
W	M H L	7/7	100
X	H L M	7/7	100
Y	H L H	7/7	100
Z	M H L	8/8	100
Moc. 1	M H L	8/8	100
Moc. 2	M H L	7/8	87
Moc. 3	M H L	8/8	100
Moc. 4	M H L	6/8	75

AVERAGE OF SIMILARITY 87 PERCENT

occur (List 1963:7). Segment G is sung in the extreme low register of the voice. The pitches sung in these circumstances are quite indistinct and I cannot be certain that the pitches offered in my transcriptions represent the contours the singers may have had in mind.

Another approach to the determination of the degree of adherence to norm would be to calculate the average of all the percentages given in the right column of Figure 17. The resultant average is 87 percent, which is well above the 75 percent I had set as the lower boundary of the norm.

I have deferred contour analysis of the Identificatory Introduction until this point. For reasons previ-ously indicated, not all the singers perform it. However, it is of interest to compare the five performances in which it is heard (Fig. 18 below). The column to the left represents the performances and subsequent columns the four groups sung.

1A and 8Fa contain the same contour in all four groups, HLM. Singer D performs a different contour than the others in the first group, singer C a different contour than the others in the fourth group. Singer C takes a breath before he completes the fourth group and sings three rather than two syllables. This variation is apparently idiosyncratic since it is heard in two performances by this singer, 3C and 6C, which were recorded on different days. I assume that the

Figure 18. Contour Analysis of the Identificatory Introduction of the Kachina Dance Song

	GROUP I	GROUP II	GROUP III	GROUP IV
1A	H L M	H L M	H L M	H L M
3C	H L M	H L M	H L M	H L H
6C	H L M	H L M	H L M	H L H
4D	M H L M	H L M	H L M	H L M
8Fa	H L M	H L M	H L M	H L M

Figure 19. Results of Contour Analysis of the Identificatory Introduction of the Kachina Dance Song

SEGMENT	MAJOR CONTOUR	RATIO	PERCENTAGE
I	H L M	4/5	80%
II	H L M	5/5	100
III	H L M	5/5	100
IV	H L M	3/5	60
		AVERAGE OF SIMILARITY	85 PERCENT

two differences in contours sung are culturally acceptable, since neither of the two Hopi who listened to the recorded performances made any comment. Except for the formal repetitions noted, and the omission of free forms or segments by singers B and D, they stated that the melody was the same in all performances.

Figure 19 offers the ratios and percentages of the contours heard in the four groups of vocables sung in the Identificatory Introduction.

The average of agreement is 85 percent. The average of agreement for the 30 lettered segments of the song in the analysis is 87 percent, which is slightly higher than that of the Identificatory Introduction. This is somewhat surprising considering the specific function of the latter. If we had eight rather than five examples, the average of agreement would perhaps be higher. Nevertheless, it does point to the fact that considerable variation can occur from our point of view without the listening Hopi feeling that either the Identificatory Introduction or the remainder of the song is not being sung correctly.

3.8.2. Comparison of Pitch Levels

In Chapter 2, I stated my hypothesis that the Hopi conceive a melody as a series of contrasting melodic contours (2.1.1, p. 5). In this chapter I have analyzed these contours and demonstrated that those sung in most segments by the different singers are much more alike than they are different. By comparing performances by the same singer we can assess the consistency of pitch level in moving from one contour to another as well as pitch relations within the contour. In Figure 15 (p. 28) I placed performances by singers B and C one immediately over the other for purposes of comparison. The intervallic relationships seen between these performances is given in schematic form in Figure 21. Performance 6C is almost always at either the same pitch level as 3C or higher. In the left margin of Figure 21, 6C is therefore placed above 3C. In the case of singer B there are three performances of the first section of the song, although the first of these, 2Ba, is incom-

plete. Thus we have two sets of comparisons in Figure 21. For the first section of the song we have 2Ba placed over 2Bb and when there is disparity in pitch level, the former is usually sung at a higher pitch than the latter. In addition we have a comparison of 7B with 2Bb for both sections of the song. 7B is almost always sung at higher level than 2B and is therefore placed above it.

Beneath the segment letters are placed groups of three numbers which are separated by hyphens. These numbers represent the intervallic relationships seen between the two performances indicated to the left. The number 1 indicates that two performances are in unison, the number 2 that the upper performance is a second higher than the lower, the number 3 that the upper is a third higher than the lower, and so forth. The first number represents the relationship between the two performances at the beginning of the segment, the third number that seen at the end of the segment. The second or middle number represents the largest interval of difference between the two segments. On occasion the performance given as the upper part of the fraction may dip below that given as the lower performance of the fraction. In this case the number representing the interval below is underlined. Should such a crossing of melodic lines occur within the segment rather than at its beginning or end, two middle numbers are given, one underlined and one not. This process is explained in Figure 20.

The simplest means of assessing the differences in pitch levels displayed in the comparisons made in Figure 21 is to list the number of intervals of each size seen. This is done in Figure 22. The numbers above the columns represent intervals, the 1 a unison, 2 a second, 3 a third, and so forth. The upper half of the figure represents all segments sung in this section. In performance 2Ba segments I-K are not sung. The lower half of the figure therefore offers the intervals seen only in segments A-H, plus L.

Since Figure 21 and the listing of intervals seen in Figure 22 are derived from pitch band notation, they cannot be considered fully accurate. The pitch band is a whole tone in width and what is written may vary

Figure 20. Examples Explaining Derivation of Intervallic Groupings in Figure 21

Figure 21. Intervallic Relationships in Performances by the Same Singer

Seg.	A	B	C	D	E	F
6C / 3C	1-1-1	1-1-1	1-1-1	2-2-2	2-2-2	2-2-2-2
2Ba / 2Bb	3-1-1	2-1-1	1-1-1	2-3-1	1-4-4	6-6-2
7B / 2Bb	2-3-3	3-4-3	4-3-3	3-2-2	3-3-3	5-3-2

	G	H	I	J	K	L
6C / 3C	1-1-1	3-3-2	1-1-1	2-1-1	1-1-1	2-5-2
2Ba / 2Bb	1-1-1	3-3-2				4-2-2
7B / 2Bb	2-5-3	2-2-2	3-6-2	2-2-2	2-2-1	1-3-1

	M	N	O	P	Q	R
6C / 3C	2-2-2-1	1-1-1	1-1-1	1-1-1	1-2-1	1-1-1
7B / 2Bb	2-6-4	4-4-4	4-4-4	3-4-4	4-4-4	4-4-4

	S	T	U	V	W	X
6C / 3C	1-1-1	1-1-1	1-1-1	1-1-1	1-1-1	1-1-1
7B / 2Bb	4-4-4	4-4-4	4-5-4	4-4-4	5-6-4	5-6-4

	Y	Z	Moc. 1	Moc. 2	Moc. 3	Moc. 4
6C / 3C	1-3-1	1-1-1	2-3-2	2-3-2	2-4-1	2-2-2
7B / 2Bb	4-4-4	4-4-4	4-5-3	3-4-2	3-4-3	3-3-3

Figure 22. Totals of Each Size Interval Seen in the First Section of Figure 21

	Segments A-L						
Intervals	1	2	3	4	5	6	Totals
6C / 3C	20	13	2		1		36
2Ba / 2Bb	12	6	4	3		2	27
7B / 2Bb	3	13	14	2	2	1	35
	Segments A-L, but Without I, J, and K						
	1	2	3	4	5	6	Totals
6C / 3C	12	12	2		1		27
2Ba / 2Bb	12	6	4	3		2	27
7B / 2Bb	3	7	13	2	2		27

as much as a second from what is actually heard, assuming that what was heard was a reasonably stable pitch rather than some sort of glide.

Thus to establish the general tone level of the section, it is best to combine the two most frequently seen intervals which, in each case, lie adjacent to each other. Concerning the upper half of Figure 22, in 6C/3C there are 20 unisons and 13 seconds. The latter figure includes seconds below, that is, those which are underlined in Figure 21 (this will hold for all future totals of seconds). Combined they form 33 of the 36 intervals found in this section. In 2Ba/2Bb there are 12 unisons and 6 seconds, which combine to form 18 out of 27 intervals.

In 7B/2Bb there are 13 seconds and 14 thirds, which combine to form 27 of the 35 intervals seen. On the basis of the frequency of intervals seen, performance 7B is obviously sung at a pitch level a second higher than 2Bb.

Looking at it from the opposite point of view, it can be seen that in 6C/3C three of 36 intervals, or 8 percent, are outside the generally established pitch level, that is, they are not unisons nor seconds or are found below the unison. In 2Ba/2Bb, nine of the 27 intervals, or 33 percent, lie outside the generally established pitch level. In 7B/2Bb, eight of 35 intervals, or 22 percent, lie outside the generally established pitch level, that is, this number and percentage of intervals are not seconds or thirds. However, it might be more equitable to transpose 7B down a step for purposes of comparison. It then would include 13 unisons and 14 seconds, to which would be added what were formerly 3 unisons and which now become seconds below. Thus the total is now 13 unisons and 17 seconds. Combined they total 30, there being only five of 35, or 14 percent, outside the generally established pitch level.

In summary, 6C/3C is the most consistent in maintaining the established common pitch level and 2Ba/2Bb is the least consistent, 7B/2Bb lying between the two but closer to the former than to the latter. The tonal relationship of 2Ba to 2Bb is therefore considerably less consistent than that of 7B to 2Bb, especially in the use of intervals larger than those employed to establish the general tonal level. This

strengthens my belief that singer B found performance 2Ba to be inadequate and therefore did not finish the meaningful portion of the section, but tacked on the vocables with which this section concludes and then began again with segment A.

Since segments I-K are omitted in performance 2Ba, it may be more equitable to compare the intervals only in the segments seen in all three comparisons. These are given in the lower half of Figure 22. Now 6C/3C has 12 unisons and 12 seconds, a total of 24 out of 27, there being only three intervals, or 11 percent, outside the established pitch level. The results of the comparison of 2Ba/2Bb remain the same, 12 unisons and 6 seconds combining to form 18 out of 27, leaving 33 percent lying outside the established general pitch level. 7B/2Bb now has seven intervals of a second and 13 of a third, combined to form 20 out of a total of 27 intervals. There are still three unisons. Transposing this comparison down a second as before, and adding the unisons as seconds below, we arrive at 23 of 27 intervals falling within the established general pitch level. The four intervals which are not form approximately 14 percent of the whole.

Comparing the above results with those achieved before, we find the number of intervals outside the established general pitch level in 6C/3C was 8 percent and is now 11 percent; 2Ba/2Bb was 33 percent and remains so; and 7B/2Bb was 14 percent and also remains so. Thus the relationships between the three comparisons when only segments A-H plus L are considered remain almost the same. 2Ba/2Bb is still much less consistent than the other two comparisons and the difference between 6C/3C and 7B/2Bb is narrowed only slightly.

In Figure 23 6C/3C has 39 unisons and 12 intervals of a second, combining to form 51 out of the total of 55 intervals. In 7B/2Bb there are eight intervals of a third and 37 intervals of a fourth, combining to form 36 out of 54 intervals. Performance 7B is obviously either a third or a fourth higher than performance 2Bb. The general pitch level of 7B in the second section of the song can therefore be considered to be approximately a tone higher than its pitch level in the first section. Transposing it down a third we have eight unisons and 37 seconds. To the latter must be added the two present

Figure 23. Totals of Each Size of Interval Seen in the Second Section of Figure 21

Segments M—Moccasin 4

	1	2	3	4	5	6	Totals
6c / 3c	39	12	3	1			55
7B / 2Bb		2	8	37	4	3	54

Figure 24. Totals of Each Size of Interval Seen in the Moccasin

	1	2	3	4	5	6	Totals
6C/3C	1	8	2	1			12
7B/2Bb		1	7	3	1		12

seconds which become seconds below. There are no unisons to consider. When 7b is transposed there are thus eight unisons and 39 seconds, combining to form 47 of 54 intervals.

Looking at the larger intervals which do not form part of the established general pitch level as derived from the great majority of the intervals, we find that in 6C/3C there are four such intervals out of a total of 55, the larger intervals thus comprising 7 percent of the total. In 7B/2Bb there are six such intervals out of 54, comprising 11 percent of the total. Thus the tonal relationship of 6C/3C and 7B/2Bb is relatively more consistent in the second section of the song than in the first. This is also evident in the greater preponderance of a single interval shown in the second section rather than the first. In the second section 6C/3C has 39 unisons out of 55 intervals, or 70 percent, while in 7B/2Bb the interval of a fourth is preponderant, there being 37 fourths out of a total of 54, which is 68 percent of the total.

In contrast, in examining the upper half of Figure 22, we find 6C/3C to have 20 unisons out of 36 intervals, or 55 percent, while 7B/2Bb has 13 seconds and 14 thirds, the preponderant thirds making up only 40 percent of the total of 35 intervals. In the lower half of Figure 22, 6C/3C has an equal number of unisons and seconds, 12 each, each equaling 44 percent of the total of 27 intervals, while in 7B/2Bb the third is preponderant, there being 13 of these intervals out of a total of 27, or 48 percent. Thus, in a number of ways, performances by singers C and B of the second section of the song are more consistent in tonal level than those in the first section. However, this is not necessarily true in the Moccasin. The totals for the different sizes of intervals given in the four groups of the Moccasin are given below in Figure 24.

In the above it can be seen that in 6C/3C there is a preponderance of seconds, and more thirds than unisons. In 7B/2Bb there are more thirds than fourths. Should we consider segments M-Z without the four groups of the Moccasin, the preponderance of unisons in 6C/3C rises to 69 percent and of fourths in 7B/2Bb to 80 percent.

3.8.3. Change of Pitch Level Between Segments

Another method of determining general pitch relationships is to check the intervals occurring between the end of one segment and the beginning of the subsequent segment. I took particular care in developing these intervals (see 2.1.4, p. 10), and although I am using pitch band notation, the actual deviation from what was heard is rarely more than a semitone. The melographs were particularly useful in checking such intervals and I referred to them frequently for this purpose. It can be noted in both Figures 25 and 26 that in his two performances singer C sings segment C at the same pitch level but the subsequent segment, D, at two different pitch levels, 6C a second higher than 3C. This can be easily seen in the pitch charts of the melograph made of the two performances. Figure 25 contrasts the latter portion of segment C and the first portion of segment D, as seen in the melographs and the transcriptions of performances 6C and 3C.

In Figure 27 the numbers represent the comparison of the interval between the last note of one segment and the first note of the next segment in the two parts. Thus when the interval between the two performances of the two segments remains the same, the relationship is expressed as 1. When there is a change in the relationship, when the interval between the two performances differs, whether by ascending or descending motion of either or both of the performances, this is indicated by 2 or 3.

Figure 26 explains the process by which these intervals are derived.

Since in Figure 27 the numbers represent change in intervallic relationship between the end of one segment and the beginning of another, the columns are identified by two segment letters separated by a hyphen, A-B, B-C, and so forth.

Figure 28 provides totals of each size interval seen in the comparisons made in Figure 27.

In the upper set of totals given in Figure 28, 6C/3C and 7B/2Bb have the same number of unisons, seconds, and thirds. 2Ba/2Bb has fewer

Figure 25. Change of Pitch Level Between Segments

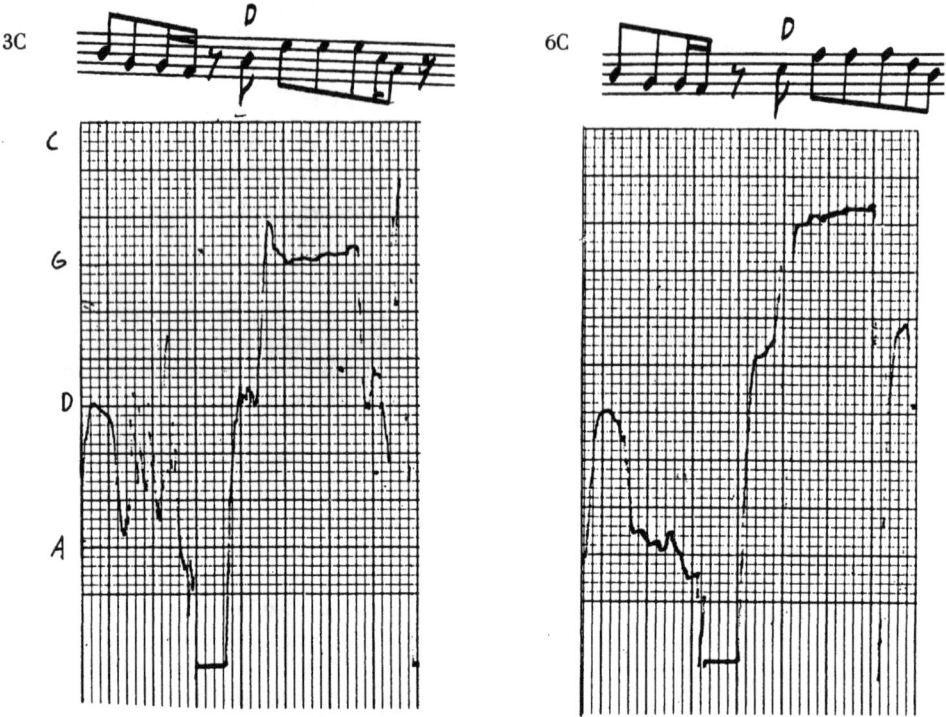

Figure 26. Explanation of the Derivation of Intervals Given in Figure 27

Figure 27. Comparison of Change in Pitch Level Between Segments

Segments A-B through L-M

	A-B	B-C	C-D	D-E	E-F	F-G	G-H
6C/3C	1	1	2	1	1	2	3
2Ba/2B	2	1	2	1	3	2	3
7B/2Bb	1	2	1	2	3	1	2

	H-I	I-J	J-X	K-L	L-M
6C/3C	2	2	1	2	1
2Ba/2Bb					
7B/2Bb	2	1	1	1	2

Segments M-N through Moccasin 4

	M-N	N-0	0-P	P-Q	Q-R	R-S	S-T
6C/3C	1	1	1	1	1	1	1
7B/2Bb	1	1	2	1	1	1	1

	T-U	U-V	V-W	W-X	X-Y	Y-Z	Z-M1
6C/3C	1	1	1	1	1	1	2
7B/2Bb	1	1	2	2	1	1	1

	M1-M2	M2-M3	M3-M4
6C/3C	1	1	2
7B/2Bb	1	2	1

unisons and seconds, but more thirds. Performance 2Ba/2Bb participates in only seven of the 12 connections made between segments. The next group of totals only includes seven segments, A-B through G-H. 6C/3C and 7B/2Bb still have more unisons and fewer thirds than 2Ba/2Bb but the latter is equal to 7B/2Bb in the number of seconds. Whereas in the first set of totals 6C/3C and 7B/2Bb were equal in number of unisons and seconds, the former now has more unisons and fewer seconds than the latter. The unison represents the closest possible maintenance of the pitch level relationship from one segment to the next. Should we rate the three performances according to the degree to which they adhere to this relationship, 6C/3C would be first, 7B/2Bb second, and 2Ba/2Bb third.

Turning to the second section of the song, we find that none of the connections between segments dis-plays the interval of a third; all are unisons or seconds. Performance 6C/3C has two more unisons and two fewer seconds than performance 7B/2Bb.

3.8.4. General Maintenance of Pitch Level

Approaching the analysis made of the maintenance of pitch level from a more general point of view, it can be seen that the cultural norm of 75 percent or larger is reached in both types of analysis, that of the intervallic relationship within the segments and that of the intervallic relationship between the end of one segment and the beginning of another. However, in most cases this norm is only reached when unisons and seconds are considered together. This is made necessary by the exigencies of pitch band notation. Figure 29 gives the percentages secured when the totals of the two most common sizes

Figure 28. Totals of Each Size Interval Found in Figure 27

First Section, A-B through L-M

Intervals	1	2	3	4	5	6	Totals
$\frac{6C}{3C}$	6	5	1				12
$\frac{2Ba}{2Bb}$	2	3	2				7
$\frac{7B}{2Bb}$	6	5	1				12

First Section, Excluding I-J through L-M

	1	2	3	4	5	6	Totals
$\frac{6C}{3C}$	4	2	1				7
$\frac{2Ba}{2Bb}$	2	3	2				7
$\frac{7B}{2Bb}$	3	3	1				7

Second Section, Including M-M through Moccasin 3-4

	1	2	3	4	5	6	Totals
$\frac{6C}{3C}$	15	2					17
$\frac{7B}{2Bb}$	13	4					17

of intervals found within a segment are combined and compared with the total of all sizes of intervals found within the segment. For ease in comparison, the totals given for 7B/2Bb represent the transpositions previously made (3.8.2). Thus only unisons and seconds are combined in Figure 29.

In Figure 29 the combination of unisons plus seconds produces a percentage that is greater than the established norm of 75 percent in both the first and second sections of the song for 6C/3C and 7B/2Bb. Whether the first section of the song is analyzed as a whole, as under the /first heading of Figure 29, or only those segments in which 2Ba/2Bb participate, segments A-H plus L, 2Ba/2Bb never reaches 75 percent while 6C/3C and 7B/2Bb always exceed this percentage. In the second section of the song, where only the interval relationships found between 6C/3C and 7B/2Bb are considered, the combined unisons and seconds form an even greater percentage of the whole, as they also do in the first and second sections of the song combined. Since performance 2Ba is an incomplete rendition of only the first section of the song, it is not considered under the latter heading.

Figure 30 is concerned with the relationship between the intervals with which one segment ends and the subsequent one begins. In no case in the first section of the song do the unisons or seconds alone display a percentage equal to that of the established norm of 75 percent. When combined the percentage is much higher than 75 percent. This is because

most of the intervals are unisons or seconds; there are very few thirds. In Figure 29, 2Ba/2Bb reaches 66 percent when unisons and seconds are combined, while in Figure 30 it reaches 71 percent. Although the differences are not very large, they are below the established norm. In the second section of the song in 6C/3C and 7B/2Bb, unisons form a percentage above 75 percent. When unisons and seconds are combined, both display 100 percent. This is because there are only unisons and seconds, and no thirds, in the second section of the song. When both first and second sections are combined, the percentage of unisons does not reach that of the established norm, although 6C/3C is closer to it than 7B/2Bb. However, when unisons and seconds are combined both reach a high of 96 percent.

The results of the analysis above fortify three previous conclusions. The first is that singer C is somewhat more consistent in maintaining the established pitch level than B; second, both singers find it easier to maintain pitch level in the second section of the song than in the first; third, performance 2B remains less consistent than the other two performances, thus strengthening my belief that the singer did not find this part of his performance adequate.

3.8.5. Durational Aspects

So far I have dealt with the pitch aspects of melody. I shall now consider its durational aspect. In

Figure 29. Percentages of the Whole Secured When the Two Most Common Intervals
Within a Compared Segment Are Combined

First Section—Segments A-L

	Total No. Intervals	Total No. Unisons and Seconds Combined	Percent of Total
$\frac{6C}{3C}$	36	33	91
$\frac{2Ba}{}$	27	18	66
$\frac{7B}{2Bb}$	35	30	85

First Section—Segments A-H plus L

$\frac{6C}{3C}$	27	24	88
$\frac{2Ba}{2Bb}$	27	18	66
$\frac{7B}{2Bb}$	27	23	85

Second Section—M-Moccasin 4

$\frac{6C}{3C}$	55	51	92
$\frac{7B}{2Bb}$	54	47	85

First and Second Sections Combined

$\frac{6C}{3C}$	91	84	92
$\frac{7B}{2B}$	89	77	86

Figure 32 I list in contrast all pitches sung which have a combined duration of a quarter note value or more. I have considered breath accents sung to the same vowel and on the same pitch to represent part of a continuum, that is, a type of sustained pitch. However, where breath accents add to the durational value of the pitch originally sung on the vowel, the numerical value representing breath accents follows plus signs. Thus $2 + 2 + 2$ expresses the situation in which the initial pitch sung to the vowel is an eighth note (representing two sixteenth notes in durational value) plus two breath accents sung on the same pitch to the same vowel, each an eighth note in length. The designation $1 + 2 + 2$ indicates that the initial syllable is only a sixteenth note in value, but is followed by two breath accents, each an eighth note in length and sung on the same pitch to the same vowel.

Figure 31 explains how the numbers in the numerical groups given in Figure 32 were arrived at.

In Figure 32 the columns represent free forms within segments. A.2 represents the second free form in segment A and U.4 the fourth free form in segment U.

Figure 33 offers in tabular form the results of the analysis made in Figure 32. As before, the figure to the left of the slash represents the most common

durational value seen and the figure to the right, the number of performances. Such ratios are given separately for performances by the First Mesa singers and those by the Third Mesa singer. They are then combined and finally offered in the form of a percentage. Thus in A.2 the same durational pattern is sung in all eight performances by the singers from the First Mesa but is sung in neither performance by the Third Mesa singer. Combined they equal 8/10 or 80 percent. In D.2 the same durational pattern is seen in four out of seven performances by the First Mesa singers and in both of the performances by the Third Mesa singer, for a ratio of 6/9 or 66 percent.

Durational patterns or single pitches with values of a quarter note or greater are seen in the various performances within only 11 segments. In four cases the concurrence is 100 percent. In two other cases the percentage is also above the established norm of 75 percent. Thus in only 6 of 11 cases does the concurrence reach the established norm. Other concurrences are quite low, two of them being in the 20 percentile range. The average of similarity is thus only 69 percent (as before this figure is secured by adding all the percentages and dividing them by the number of items analyzed, in this case 11). This does

Figure 30. Percentages of the Whole of Intervallic Relationships Between Segments

First Section—Segments A-B through L-M

	Total No. Intervals	Unisons	%	Seconds	%	Unisons and Seconds	%
6C / 3C	12	6	50	5	41	11	91
2Ba / 2Bb	7	2	28	3	42	5	71
7B / 2Bb	12	6	50	5	41	11	91

First Section—Segments A-B through G-H

6C / 3C	7	4	57	2	28	6	85
2Ba / 2Bb	7	2	28	3	42	5	71
7B / 2Bb	7	3	42	3	42	6	85

Second Section—Segments M-N Through Moccasin 3-4

6C / 3C	17	15	88	2	11	17	100
7B / 2Bb	17	13	76	4	23	17	100

First and Second Sections Combined

6C / 3C	29	21	72	7	24	28	96
7B / 2Bb	29	19	65	9	31	28	96

not reach the established norm but is not very far below it. Nevertheless the average of similarity as far as sustained pitches are concerned is lower than that found in contour analysis. Greater concurrence might have been secured if I had established the durational value of a dotted eighth as the cutoff point rather than a quarter note. However, the pulse is an eighth note in duration and it would seem a pitch should encompass at least two pulses to be considered to exhibit significant length. Had the song been accompanied by idiophones, as in actual performance, the percentage of concurrence might well have been higher.

3.9. Comparison of the Sung Texts

In Figure 14 I gave two spoken versions of the meaningful text of the kachina dance song, one for the First Mesa and one for the Third Mesa, plus their translations into English. In the subsequent pages the points at which these two versions differ were discussed (3.5). Figure 34 provides a comparison of all sung texts of the song including all vocables, as well as the phones added to the meaningful text. To facilitate the comparisons being made, I include spoken versions I and III, respectively, above and below

the sung texts. The sung performances and spoken versions are identified to the left, the segments above.

3.10. Analysis of the Meaningful Portions of the Texts

3.10.1. Comparison of Words or Free Forms

I shall first consider the meaningful portions of the sung text. If we consider free forms only, and omit consideration of the changes which take place within the free forms, the sung versions generally reflect their relationship with the two spoken versions. Thus the free forms sung by the First Mesa singers A-E are those seen in spoken version I and those by singer F, from the Third Mesa, are those seen in spoken version III. In segments A and B singers A-E sing *iyaaha*, as seen in version I, and singer F sings *haw uma*, as seen in version III. Singers A-E also begin the free form *taawanawita* in segment I, as seen in version I, singer F in segment G, as seen in version III. Singers A-D sing *imömu* in segment H, singer F omits this and it thus does not appear in version III. Contrariwise, in segment S singer F sings a fourth

Figure 31. Examples Explaining Analytic Process Employed in Figure 32

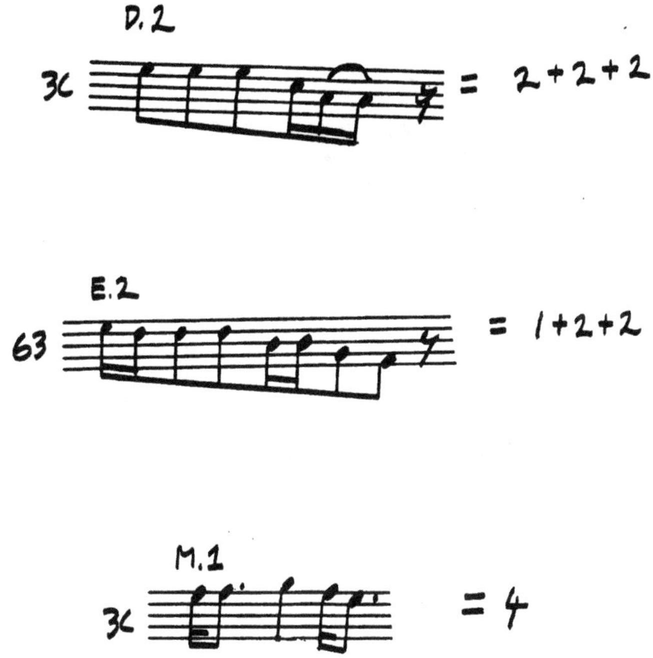

free form, *pay*, as seen in version III. This is not sung by singers A-E and thus does not appear in version I. (The reader should again note that I am dealing with full free forms without considering any internal modifications which may have occurred.)

The exceptions to the above are listed below:

1. There are two cases where performance 1A differs from all other performances recorded at the First Mesa. (It should be remembered that 1A was recorded in the 1920s and the remainder in 1960.) In performance 1A the third free form of segment N is *pituqw·ö*, while in the remainder of the performances from First Mesa it is *ökeqw·ö*. What is given in version I is what is found in the majority of First Mesa performances. However, the free form in 1A is that seen in 8F and therefore in version III. The two free forms differ in number, one being dual and the other plural.

The second case is problematical. In segment K the singer of 1A sings *liiƚa*, which according to my second Hopi translator is a Zuni word meaning "right here." All other singers perform vocables at this point. (This phenomenon is discussed in some detail on p. 25, Note 4).

2. There are two cases where entire free forms found in the spoken version I are omitted by singers from the First Mesa. In performance 2Ba the singer omits five free forms in a row. These are the four free forms in segment I plus the free form *taawanawita*, which begins in segment I and continues through the first part of segment K. In performance 4D two free forms, *uysonaq* and *itahkway* are omitted. It has been previously noted that 5E is not a complete performance. By mistake the singer moves from segment C to segment P and ends with the first part of the first free form of segment Q. He thus omits segments D-O, the remainder of segment Q, and segments R-Z.

3.10.2. Non-Phonemic Variation of the Meaningful Texts

I have previously discussed the non-phonemic disparities found between the two spoken versions of the text. These are changes which apparently do not alter meaning. Such differences were listed under Substitutions and Elisions/Additions in 3.6.2a-b. I will now discuss the non-phonemic variation found in the meaningful portions of the sung performances of the text which do not conform with either or both of the spoken versions. Three types of variation will be considered: substitution, elision, and addition. Each letter will be considered one phone. Thus, with one exception, which will be discussed below, diph-

Figure 32. Comparison of Sustained Pitches in the Kachina Dance Song

PERFORMANCE SEGMENT	1A	3C	6C	2Ba	2Bb	7B	4D	5E	8Fa	8Fb
A.2	2+2+2	2+2+2	2+2+2	2+2+2	2+2+2	2+2+2	2+2+2	2+2+2	2+2+2 +2+2	2+2+2 +2+2
D.2	1+2+2	2+2+2	2+2+2	2+2+2	2+2+1	2+2+1	2+2+2		2+2+2	2+2+2
E.2	1+2+2	1+2+2	1+2+2	1+2+2	1+2+2	1+2+2	1+2+2		1+2	2+2+2
I.5		2+2					2+2			
M.1	4	4								
P.1	8	8	8		8	8	12	6		8
R.1	2+2	2+2	2+2		2+2	2+2	2+2			2+2
T.1	2+2	2+2	2+2		2+2	2+2	2+2			2+2
U.4	2+2	2+2	2+2		2+2	2+2	2+2			2+2
W.1	8	6	7			6	6			2+2
Y.1	2+2	2+2	2+2		2+2	2+2	2+2			2+2

Figure 33. Results of Analysis of Durational Values in Figure 32

	A.2	D.2	E.2	I.5	M.1	P.1	R.1	T.1	U.4	W.1	Y.1
1ST MESA	8/8	4/7	7/7	2/6	2/6	4/7	6/6	6/6	6/6	3/6	6/6
3RD MESA	0/2	2/2	0/2	0/2	0/1	0/1	1/1	1/1	1/1	0/1	1/1
TOTALS	8/10	6/9	7/9	2/8	2/7	4/8	7/7	7/7	7/7	3/7	7/7
PERCENT	80	66	77	25	28	50	100	100	100	42	100

AVERAGE OF SIMILARITY 69 PERCENT

thongs will be considered to consist of two separate phones. In the tabulations below each letter or phone or, rather, the space it occupies, will be counted only once. For example, in O.2 a group of three letters ʾat, is elided at the end of the free form. The glottal stop is listed in Figure 38, which is concerned with the elision of glottal stops, and the at in Figure 39, in which elision of all other types of letters are listed. Similarly, although the change in phone may represent more than one function, only one will be counted. For example, also in O.2, the glottal stop in the spoken version is replaced in the sung version by a *y*. This is listed in Figure 37, Other Substitutions, as a *y* substituted for a glottal stop. Although a glottal stop has obviously been elided, it is not so listed in Figure 38.

3.10.2a. Substitutions

Figure 35 lists the most common phonemic variation occurring in the sung performance, *ey* for *i*. In the great majority of the cases the change is not from a single vowel *i* to the diphthong *ey*, but to a high, rounded *e* like that heard in the German word *schnee*. In the song text *e* already has a different phonemic meaning and *e* and *y* appear only once in juxtaposition in the spoken text, in segment U in the free form

pölöneyang. Yang is given as a separate word in Seaman's Dictionary, meaning "here," etc. The preceding *ne* is apparently a prefix.

In the following discussion the diphthong *ey* therefore represents in most cases the *e* heard in the German word *schnee* but occasionally the Hopi *e*, pronounced like the *e* in the English word "let," to which the glide *y* has been added. The two sounds are very similar and are not differentiated here. Neither apparently provides a phonemic contrast in Hopi. It thus should be noted that the diphthong *ey* is exceptional in that it is counted as one phone rather than two.

Figure 35 has four headings. That to the left represents location, the two to the right of this the sung performances from First Mesa compared with spoken version I, and the Third Mesa sung performance compared with spoken version III. In both cases the numbers represent instances of *ey* substituted in the sung performances for the *i* found in the spoken version. The fourth column offers totals of the previous two.

This substitution is most likely to occur in initial position and least likely to occur in medial position. This applies to performances by both First Mesa and Third Mesa singers.

Figure 34. Comparison of the Sung and Spoken Texts of the Kachina Dance Song

Identificatory Introduction

1A	hu yu hay yey	hey yey hey yey	hey yə hay yay	hey yey hey
3C	hu yu hey ye hey	hey yey hey yey	hay yae hay ye yay	hay yey he ye yey
6C	hu yu hey ye hay	hey yey hey yey	hay yae hey ye yay	hay yey he ye yey
4D	a ha ya ya hay	hey yey yey hey	hey yay yay hay	hey yey yey
8Fa	ha ya ya ya	hey yey yey	haw yaw yaw yaw	hey hey hey

	A	B	C	D	E
I	iyaaha	imöyhoyatu	iyaaha	imömu	umuhkway
1A	eyyaaha	imöy'ehoya'yatu'yu'yu	eyyaaha	imömu'yu	umuhkway'yay
3C	eyyaaha	imöyhoya'yatu'yu'yu	eyyaaha	imömu	umuhkway'yay
6C	eyyaaha	imöyhoya'yatu'yu'yu	eyyaaha	imömu	umuhkway'yay
2Ba	eyyaaha	imöyhoyatu'yey'ye	eyyaaha	imömu'yu	umuhkway'yay
2Bb	eyyaaha	imöyhoyata'yey'ye	eyyaaha	imömu'yu	umuhkway'yay
7B	eyyaaha	imöyhoyatu'yu'yu	eyyaaha	imömu'yu	umuhkway'yay
4D	eyyaaha	imöyhoyatu'u'yu	eyyaaha	imömu	umuhkway'ay
5E	eyyaaha	imöyhoyatu'yu'yu	eyyaaha	imömu	umukway
8Fa	haw uma	eymöyhoyatu'u'u'u'u	haw uma	eymömu	
8Fb	haw uma	eymöyhoyatu'u'u'u'u	haw uma	eymömu'yu	umuuhkway'yay
III	haw uma	imöyhoyatu	haw uma	imömu	umuukway

	D			E		F
I	uuyiyat	ang	yookva	ang	paatalawa	aw
1A	uuyey	ang	yoo'o'okway	ang	paa'yay'yaytalawvay	aw
3C	uuyey	ang	yoo'o'okvay	ang	paa'yay'yaytalawvay	aw
6C	uuyey	ang	yoo'o'okvay	ang	paa'yay'yaytalawvay	aw
2Ba	uuyey	ang	yoo'o'okuvay	ang	paa'yay'yaytalawvay	aw
2Bb	uuyey	ang	yoo'o'okuvay	ang	paa'yay'yaytalawvay	aw
7B	uuyey	ang	yoo'o'okuvay'ya	ang	paa'yay'talawyy	aw
4D	uuyey	ang	yoo'o'okuva	ang	paa'yay'yaytalawvay	aw
5E	uuyeyya	ang				
8Fa	uuyeyyat	ang	yo'o'okva'ya	qw ang	paa'latalawvay	aw
8Fb	uuyeyyat	ta ang	yo'o'ova'ya	qw ang	paa'a'atalawvay	aw
III	uuyiyat	ang	yokva	ang	paatalawva	aw

	G		H		I
I	uma	munlalay__toni		imömu	umuhkway
1A	umay'yay	munlalay__toney	hay yay hay yay yaw	imömu	umuhkway'yay
3C	uma'ye	munlalay__toney	ha la ho o o	imömu	umuhkway
6C	uma'æ	munlalay__toney	ha la ho o o	himomu	umuhkivay
2Ba	umay'lay	munlalay__toney	hay yay hay yay yaw	imömu	
2Bb	umay'yay	munlalay__toney	hay yay hay yay yaw	imömu	umuhkway
7B	umay'yay	munlalay__toney	hay yay hay yay yaw	imömu	umuhkway
4D	uma	munlalay__toney	hay yey wo o o	imömu	umukway
8Fa	uma	munlalay__toney	taawa'ya'ya_____	nawita	umuukway
8Fb	uma'ya	munlalay__toney	taa'yawa'ya'ya_____	nawita	umuukway
III	uma	munlalay__toni	taawa_____	nawita	umuukway

				J	K
I	uma	amum	momortoni	taa____wa	nawita
1A	uma	amum	momortoney	taay____wa'ya'ya	nawita'la
3C	uma	amum	momortoney	taa'la____wa'la'la	nawita'la
6C	uma	amum	momortoney	taa____wal'a'la	nawita'la
2Ba					
2Bb	uma	amum	momortoney	taa____wa'yay'yay	nawit'a'la
7B	uma	amum	momortoney	taa____wa'lal'lal	nawita'la
4D	uma	amum	momortoney	taa'yay____way'yay'yay	nawita'la
8Fa	uma	amum	momotoney	hey ye hey hæy____hey hæy	
8Fb	uma	amum	momortoney	lay yay_____hey yay yey	
III	uma	amum	momortoni		

Figure 34. (Continued)

	L			M	
I	liiƛa			itahso	itahkway
1A	liiƛa	hiƛiyi	he yey ta ta ta	eytaso	eytakway'yay
3C	ley yey	hey yey yay	hi yey na yəm	eytaso	eytahkway'yay
6C	ley yey	hey yey ye	hi hey na əm	heytaso	eytahkway'yay
2Ba	ney	hey yey yey	ey hey tay əm		
2Bb	ley	ey yey yey	ey hey ta m	eytaso	eytahkway'yay
7B	ley yey	ye yey yey	ey hey la m	eytahso	eytahkway'yay
4D	ley yey	hey m m	ey hay tay yay yay	eytahso	eytahkway
8Fa	hæy		ey hey la m		
8Fb	hay hey		la le m	eaytaaso	eytaakway'ay
III				itaaso	itaakway

	N			O		
I	uuyiyat	itamuy	aw	ökiqw'ö	itahkway	uuyi'at
1A	uuyeyyat	eytamu	aw	pituq'wö	eytahkway'yay	uuyeyyat
3C	uuyeyyat	eytamu	aw	ökeqw'ö	eytahkway'yay	uuyeya
6C	uuyeyyat	eytamu	aw	ökeq'wö	eytahkway'yay	uuyeya
2Bb	uuyey	eytahmu	aw	ökeq'wö	eytahkawy'yay	uuyey
7B	uuye	eytahmu	aw	ökeqw'ö	eytahkway'yay	uuyey
4D	uuyeyyat	eytahmu	aw	ökeqw'ö		uuyey
8Fb	uuyeyyat	eytamuy	aw	pituqw'ö	eytaakway'ay	uuyeyyat
III	uuyiyat	itamuy	aw	pituqw'ö	itaakway	uuyi'at

	P	Q				
I	kuwan'ewsoniwa	itamu	ang	uysonaq	waymakyanw	taymaqw
1A	kuwan'ewsoniway	eytamu	ang	uysonaq	waymakyang	tay'aymaq
3C	kuwan'ewsoniway	eytamu	ang	uysonaq	waymakyang	tayma
6C	kuwan'ewsoniway	eytamu	ang	uysona	waymakyang	tayma
2Bb	kuwan'ewsoniway	itamu	ang	uysonaq	waymak	taymaq
7B	kuwan'ewsoniway	itamu	ang	uysonaq	waymakyang	tayma
4D	kuwan'ewsoniway	itamu	ang		wayma	tayma
5E	kuwan'ewsoniwa	ita				
8Fb	kuwan'ewsoniway	eytamuy	ang	uysonaq	waymakyang	taymaq
III	kuwan'ewsoniwa	itamuy	ang	uysonaq	waymakyang	taymaqw

	R	S				T
I	sipepetota	pu'	ang	peehu		sivöwiwyungma
1A	sipepeytotay'yay	pu'	ang	peeyhu		sivöwiwyungmay'yay
3C	hipepeytotay'yay	pu	ang	peeyhu		sivöwiwyungmay'yey
6C	sipepeytotay'yay	pu	ang	peeyhu		sivöwiwyungmay'yey
2Bb	sipepeytotay'yay	pu'	ang	peeyhu'yu		sivöwiwyungmay'ya
7B	sipepeytotay'yay	pu?	ang	peeyhu'yu		sivöwiwyungmay'yay
4D	sipepeytotay'yay	pu'	ang	peeyhu		sivöwiwyungmay'yay
8Fb	silpepeytota'ya	pu'	ang	peey'yeyhu	pa	sivöwiwyungway'yay
III	silpepetota	pu'	ang	peehu	pay	sivöwiwyungma

	U				V	
I	kaaway'uyi'at	melon'uyi'at	pölöneyang	hotam'iwta	ahaw	itupko
1A	kawayuiat	melonuiat	pölöneya	hotamiwtay'yay	ahaw	eytupko
3C	kawayuiat	melonuiat	pölöneya	hotamiwtay'ley	ahaw	eytupko
6C	kawayuiat	melonuiat	pölöneya	hotamiwtay'ley	ahaw	eytupko
2Bb	kawayuiat	melonui	pölöneyang	hotamiwtay'ley	ahaw	eytupko
7B	kawayuiat	melonui	pölöneyang	hotamiwtay'ay	ahaw	eytupko
4D	kawayuiat	melonui	pölöneyang	hotamiwtay'yay	ahaw	eytupko
8Fb	kawayuiat	melonuiat	pölöneyang	hotamiwtay'yay	awhaw	eytupko
III	kaway'uyi'at	melon'uyi'at	pölöneyang	hotam'iwta	ahhaw	itupko

Figure 34. *(Continued)*

	W	X			Y
I	owi	oovi	itam	hahlayi	itahso'
1a	owey'ey'ey'ey'ey	oovey	itam	hay'yayna'yayey	eytahso'o
3C	owey'ey'ey'ey'ey	oovi	eytam	ha'yanay'yayyay	eytahso'o
6C	owe'ey'ey'ey'ey	oovi	eytam	ha'yanay'yayyay	eytahso'o
2Bb	owey'ey'ey'ey'ey'ey'ey	oovi	eytam	ha'yana'yayey	eytahso'o
7B	owey'ey'yey'ysy'yey	oovi	eytam	ha'yana'yayey	eytahso'o
4D	owey'yey'yey'yey	oovi	eytam	ha'yal'a'yayey	eytahso'o
8Fb	owey'ey'ey'ey'yey'yey'yey'yey	oovi	eytam	haa'yala'yayey	eytahso'o
III	owi	oovi	itam	haalayi	itaaso'

	Z			Moc 1
I	is haw	is uni	askwali	
1A	es haw	es uney	askwaley'ey'yey	ha ya hu hu ya vay
3C	es haw	es uney	askwaley'ey'yey	ha ha hǝl hal a we
6C	es haw	es uney	askwaley'ey'yey	ha lǝ ha lǝ hal la ley
2Bb	es haw	es uney	askwaley'ey'yey	a ha a hal el
7B	es haw	es uney	askwaley'yey'yey	a ha lal hal lal ley
4D	es haw	es uney	askwaley'ey'ey	a ha a ha lal la
8Fb	es haw	es uney	askwaley'yey'yey	aw aw haw yaw y
8Fc	es haw	es uney	askwaley'yey'yey'yey	haw aw haw yaw ya ey
III	is haw	is uni	askwali	

	Moc. 2	Moc. 3	Moc. 4
I			
1A	ha ya hay hay ay ey	hey ey hey hey ey ey	hey ey hey ey
3C	a ha ha ha lal	hey ey ey hey ey ey ǝ	hey æ hey æ
6C	hal a ha lal	hey e hey hey æ yæ	hey æ hey æ
2Bb	a ha al ha la	ey ey hey ey e y	hey æ hey æ
7B	a ha al hal lal lǝ	i hi yey hey yey yey	hey ye hey y
4D	ey hay yey hey yey lǝ lǝ	a ha a hal la la lay lay	la la lay
8Fb	a ha haw a yaw ya	hey yǝ hey yǝ hey yǝ	ha hey ye hey ym
8FC	aw a haw aw ay	hey ey ey hey æ ye æ	he ey ya he ey
			ya he ey ya

	Moc. 5		
4D	ho u ho u ho o way	ey hey yey hey yey yey	hey ye hey ye

Notes

1. A free form extending through more than one segment is indicated by underlining connecting the parts of the free form. However, the parts of the free form found in subsequent segments are analyzed as separate free forms. Thus in spoken version I, the free form *taawanawita* begins in segment I and continues through J and K. It is, therefore, counted as three separate free forms, *taa*, *wa*, and *nawita* in the subsequent analysis.

2. Additions to the meaningful text of vowels or syllables are also underlined, when they contain vowels. Additions consisting only of consonants are not underlined.

In Figure 36 I present the number of times the vowel *i* would have appeared in the sung performances of the meaningful text in Figure 34, if the First Mesa singers had duplicated exactly what is seen in spoken version I and the Third Mesa singer had duplicated exactly what is seen in spoken version III, and neither had at times substituted an *ey* as seen in Figure 35, or *a* or *e* for *i* as seen in Figure 37.

When the figures given at the bottom of Figure 35 are compared with those given in Figure 36, it will be seen that there is some change in the ratio between the totals in medial and final position. In Figure 35 the order according to size of number is initial, final, and medial. In Figure 36 the initial position still displays the largest total, but the order of the final and medial is reversed; there being a larger total for medial position than for final position. When the grand totals in each figure are compared, we find *ey* was substituted for *i* 131 times of a possible 252 cases, or 51 percent of the time.

Figure 37 lists the other substitutions of phones made in the sung performances when compared with

Figure 35. Lists of Substitutions of *ey* for *i*
(Plus Summary Totals)

Initial Position

Location	1st Mesa ey	3rd Mesa ey	Totals ey
A.1.1	8	0	8
A.2.1	0	2	2
B.1.1	8	0	8
B.2.1	0	2	2
M.1.1	6	1	7
M.2.1	6	1	7
N.1.1	6	1	7
O.1.1	5	1	6
Q.1.1	3	1	4
V.2.1	6	1	7
X.2.1	5	1	6
Y.1.1	6	1	7

Medial Position

Location	1st Mesa ey	3rd Mesa ey	Totals ey
C.2.4	8	2	10
M.3.4	5	1	6
O.2.4	6	1	7

Final Position

Location	1st Mesa ey	3rd Mesa ey	Totals ey
C.1.4	7	2	9
W.1.3	5	1	6
X.1.4	1	0	1
X.3.7	4	1	5
Z.2.5	6	2	8
Z.3.7	6	2	8

SUMMARY OF TOTALS

Position	1st Mesa	3rd Mesa	Totals
Initial	59	12	71
Medial	19	4	23
Final	29	8	37
TOTALS	107	24	131

Figure 36. Number of Times the Vowel *i* Would
Have Appeared If no Substitutions Had Been Made

Position	1st Mesa	3rd Mesa	Totals
Initial	93	16	109
Medial	75	14	89
Final	43	11	54
TOTALS	211	41	252

the spoken version. The organization of the figure is
the same as that of Figure 35.

The distribution here as far as position is concerned again is different. The final position is now
the largest, the initial position second in size, and
the medial position quite small in number, 5.

In Figure 37 there are 13 substitutions of *e* for *i*,
and two substitutions of *a* for *i*, a total of 15 other

Figure 37. Other Substitutions of Phones in the
Sung Performances (Plus Summary of Totals)

Initial Position

Location	1st Mesa e for i	3rd Mesa e for i	Totals e for i
Z.1.1	5	2	7
Z.2.1	5	2	7
	h for s	h for s	h for s
R.1.1	1	0	1

Medial Position

Location	1st Mesa e for i	3rd Mesa e for i	Totals e for i
N.3.3	5	0	5
M.3.4	1	0	1
	n for l	n for l	n for l
S.3.4	5	0	5
	w for h	w for h	w for h
V.1.2	1	0	1
	w for v	w for v	w for v
D.2.5	1	0	1
	y for h	y for h	y for h
X.3.3	1	0	1
	y for '	y for '	y for '
O.2.5	1	1	2

Final Position

Location	1st Mesa a for i	3rd Mesa a for i	Totals a for i
X.3.7	2	0	2
	e for i	e for i	e for i
W.1.3	1	0	1

SUMMARY OF TOTALS

Position	1st Mesa	3rd Mesa	Totals
Initial	11	4	15
Medial	15	1	16
Final	3	0	3
TOTALS	29	5	34

substitutions for *i*. If we add the 15 to the 131 times
that *ey* is substituted for *i*, we have a total of 146
cases in which another vowel is substituted for *i* out
of the possible 252 cases in which the *i* could have
appeared, or 57 percent of the time.

I should now like to determine how often substitutions occur in the sung performances when they are
compared with the spoken versions. As far as First
Mesa performances are concerned, 3C, 6C, 2Bb,
and 7B have the same number of letters as spoken
version I, 348. 1A substitutes the verb *pituqwꞏö* instead of *ökiqwꞏö* and therefore has one more letter,
349. Performance 4D omits two full free forms and
thus has 333 letters. Both 2Ba and 5E are incomplete, the first containing only 85 of the 120 letters
found in spoken version I in segments A-L whereas
5E has only 61 out of the total of 348 meaningful
phones found in spoken version I. The total number

sung by the First Mesa singers is therefore 2,220. In Figure 35 there are 107 substitutions in First Mesa performances and 29 in Figure 37, a total of 136. The percentage of substitutions made by the First Mesa singers is therefore quite small, 6 percent.

Following the same process, I find that 8Fb sings all the phones found in spoken version III, 346. 8Fa sings all meaningful phones found in segments A-L of version III, 115. 8FC, which repeats segment Z only, contains 17. The total number of phones sung by singer F is therefore 478. Singer 8F makes 24 substitutions in Figure 35 and five in Figure 37, a total of 29. The percentage of substitutions made by singer 8F is therefore also 6 percent.

3.10.2b. Elisions

I now move to elisions rather than substitutions. Figure 38 lists and summarizes the pronouncing and eliding of glottal stops.

The glottal stop (see 2.2.7) appears in the transcribed spoken versions only in medial and final positions, but is much more frequent in the former. Compared with what they would have sung had they followed the spoken version I, the singers of the First Mesa elided 43 out of 61 glottal stops, or 70 percent. Following the same process, it can be seen that the

Third Mesa singer elides 66 percent of the glottal stops. When the two are combined, the percentage of elision is 68.

It should be noted that in the main part of Figure 39 the figures for elisions in final position represent the number of occurrences of an elision. In the summary totals, the figures represent instead the total number of letters elided, not the number of times the elisions took place. In the medial elisions only one letter is elided at any one time. It should also be noted that in the final position there are 38 occurrences of elisions but only 27 rests. Since each elision is not followed by a rest, it follows that not all elisions occur because the singer has run out of breath.

The most common medial elisions are of *h* and *y*, being about equal in number, 12 and 14, and combined they outnumber all other elisions found in medial position. The most common final elision is either all or part of *yat*, the modifying third person singular possessive pronoun, which in almost all cases follows the *uuyi* which means plants or corn and which also follows the specific mention of plants such as *melon* (muskmelon) and *kaway* (watermelon).

Combining the elisions of glottal stops by the First Mesa (Fig. 38) and the elisions for the First Mesa as found in the Summary of Totals (Fig. 39) there is a

Figure 38. Frequency of Performance of the Glottal Stop in the Sung Performances Compared to the Spoken Versions

Medial Position

Location	1st Mesa		3rd Mesa		Totals	
	Elided	Pronounced	Elided	Pronounced	Elided	Pronounced
N.3.6/7	0	6	0	1	0	7
O.2.5	5	0	0	0	5	0
P.1.6	0	7	0	1	0	8
U.1.6	6	0	1	0	7	0
U.1.10	6	0	1	0	7	0
U.2.6	6	0	1	0	7	0
U.2.10	6	0	1	0	7	0
U.4.6	6	0	1	0	7	0

Final Position

Location	1st Mesa		3rd Mesa		Totals	
	Elided	Pronounced	Elided	Pronounced	Elided	Pronounced
S.1.3	2	4	0	1	2	5
Y.1.7	6	0	1	0	7	0

SUMMARY OF TOTALS

Position	1st Mesa		3rd Mesa		Totals	
	Elided	Pronounced	Elided	Pronounced	Elided	Pronounced
Medial	35	13	5	2	40	15
Final	8	4	1	1	9	5
TOTALS	43	17	6	3	49	20

Figure 39. Other Elisions

Medial Position

Location	1st Mesa	3rd Mesa	Totals
	h̲	h̲	h̲
C.1.4	1	0	1
I.1.4	1	0	1
M.1.4	4	0	4
M.2.4	1	0	1
X.3.3	5	0	5
	k̲	k̲	k̲
D.2.3/4	0	1	1
	r̲	r̲	r̲
I.4.5	0	1	1
	y̲	y̲	y̲
U.1.8	6	1	7
U.2.8	6	1	7

Final Position

Location	1st Mesa	3rd Mesa	Totals	No. of Rests
	a̲t	a̲t	a̲t	a̲t
0.2.6-7	3	0	3	3
U.2.11-12	3	0	3	3
	kyangw	kyangw	kyangw	kyangw
Q.4.6-11	1	0	1	1
	mu̲	mu̲	mu̲	mu̲
Q.1.5-6	1	0	1	0
	ng̲	ng̲	ng̲	ng̲
U.3.9-10	3	0	3	2
	q̲	q̲	q̲	q̲
Q.3.7	1	0	1	0
	qw̲	qw̲	qw̲	qw̲
Q.5.6-7	4	0	4	4
	t̲	t̲	t̲	t̲
C.2.7	1	0	1	1
0.2.7	2	0	2	2
	w̲	w̲	w̲	w̲
Q.4.11	4	1	5	0
Q.5.7	2	1	3	2
	y̲	y̲	y̲	y̲
S.4.3	0	1	1	0
	yangw	yangw	yangw	yangw
Q.4.7-11	1	0	1	1
	yat	yat	yat	yat
C.2.5-7	7	0	7	6
M.3.5-7	2	0	2	2

SUMMARY OF TOTALS

Position	1st Mesa	3rd Mesa	Totals	No. of Rests
Medial	24	4	28	0
Final	76	3	79	27
TOTALS	100	7	107	27

grand total of 143 elisions. Comparing this number with the 2,220 phones sung by the First Mesa singers, it will be found that elisions occurred in the First Mesa performances 6 percent of the time. Following the same procedure for the Third Mesa performances, we secure a total of 14 elisions out of 478

phones sung or 2.9 percent. Combining First and Third mesa performances secures a total 157 elisions, which is 5.8 percent of the 2,698 phones sung.

3.10.2c. Combining Substitutions and Elisions

I shall now combine the substitutions and elisions to ascertain what percentage of the total phones sung these modifications represent. The First Mesa singers made a total of 279 substitutions and elisions, which is 12 percent of the 2,220 phones sung. The combined number of substitutions and elisions by the Third Mesa singer is 42 out of a total of 478 phones sung, or 8.9 percent. It can thus be seen that on a percentage basis a larger number of modifications of this type were made by the First Mesa singers than the singer from the Third Mesa. Combining the figures for First Mesa and Third Mesa, we arrive at a total of 321 substitutions and elisions. The total number of phones sung by the two groups of singers is 2,698. The percentage of substitutions and elisions is 11 percent. This compares with 57 percent of substitutions of *ey*, *e*, or *a* for the vowel *i* and 71 percent for the elision of glottal stops.

3.10.2d. Additions

If a letter or letters are added which are not found in the meaningful text in the spoken versions, these are considered additions. In Figure 34 additions to meaningful words were underlined only when they contain a vowel and thus could be considered a syllable. In Figures 38 and 39 all are underlined for ease in reading the tables.

The most common addition is that of a *y* to the final *a* of a free form. Such a final *a* may be followed by breath accents and still be considered the final vowel of the free form since it is that when the free form is spoken. For example, in *umay'yay* of F.2 the fourth letter, *y*, is considered an addition to the free form *uma*.

In order to derive a percentage of the occurrence of this phenomenon, I have also counted the number of times in which the final *a* of the free form is not modified by the addition of a *y*. This occurs 43 times in the performances by the First Mesa singers and 15 times in performances by the Third Mesa singer, or a total of 58. If for the First Mesa we combine the 45 times the final *a* of the free form is followed by a *y* with the 43 times in which it is not, this produces us

Figure 40. Table of *y* Added to *a* in Final Position

Location	1st Mesa	3rd Mesa	Totals
D.2.5/6x	6	0	6
E.2.9x	7	2	9
F.2.3x	4	0	4
I.5.3x	1	0	1
J.1.2x	1	0	1
P.1.14x	6	1	7
R.1.10/11x	6	0	6
T.1.13x	6	1	7
U.4.10x	6	1	7
X.3.7	2	0	2
TOTALS	45	5	50

a total of 88. Thus in the First Mesa performances a *y* is added to the final *a* 50 percent of the time. In the performances by the Third Mesa singer, the *y* is added to the final *a* five times, and not 15 times. The *y* is thus added 25 percent of the time. Compiling the occurrences in performances by the singers from both the First and Third Mesas yields 49 cases in which the *y* is added to the final *a* and 58 cases in which it is not, for a total of 107. Thus in the entire corpus *y* is added after the *a* 45 percent of the time.

Figure 41 lists the other additions heard and seen in the sung performances.

The additions are not very large in number. Combining the 27 additions in Figure 41 with the 49 in Figure 40 results in a total of only 76 added letters.

Figure 41. Other Additions

	Initial Position		
Location	1st Mesa	3rd Mesa	Totals
	h	h	h
H.1.x1	1	0	1
M.1.x1	1	0	1
R.1.x1	1	0	1
	qw	qw	qw
E.1.xx1	0	2	2
	ta	ta	ta
D.1.xx1	0	1	1
	Medial Position		
Location	1st Mesa	3rd Mesa	Totals
	h	h	
N.1.3x	3	0	3
	u	u	u
D.2.3/4x	4	0	4
	y	y	y
R.1.6/7x	6	1	7
S.3.3x	6	1	7
SUMMARY OF TOTALS			
Position	1st Mesa	3rd Mesa	Totals
Initial	3	3	6
Medial	19	2	21
TOTALS	22	5	27

This includes both First and Third Mesas. The additions comprise only 2 percent to the total number of phones sung.

3.10.3. The Lexically Meaningless Phones

We have now completed our consideration of the meaningful text of the *kachina* dance song. There are three types of lexically meaningless phones still to be considered: breath accents, vocables, and symbolic vocables.

3.10.3a. Breath Accents

As previously noted, the Hopi singing style, especially in their dance songs, is characterized by a pulsation of the diaphragm which occurs on almost every beat. Thus a syllable which is carried forward for more than one beat is not usually sustained, but rather is reiterated by means of the diaphragmatic pulsation. Exceptions occur only when the syllable to be lengthened is being sung in such a high register that the production of the normal pulsation of the diaphragm is very difficult. For example, see performance 1A, segment P.1.

The breath accent is a rather complex phenomenon. If the syllable to be continued ends with a vowel, the following breath accent or accents may consist of a reiteration of only this vowel, but this is rare. In most cases some type of consonant is inserted before the continued vowel and in many cases after the vowel as well. The syllable may also be lengthened by more than one breath accent and at times the vowel itself may be changed. Nor will the carrying forward or lengthening of the syllable necessarily take place on the same pitch as it was initially sung. In addition, both the syllable to be carried forward and the breath accents which lengthen it may be sung to more than one pitch. A striking example of a combination of these phenomena is seen in segment W in the extension of the second syllable of *owey* into a veritable melisma.

In Figure 42 breath accents have been listed primarily according to two characteristics. The first is whether or not they are sung on the same vowel as the meaningful syllable they follow. The second is whether or not they are sung on the same pitch as the syllable they follow. Determining if the breath accent is sung on the same vowel of the syllable it follows is easy. It is more difficult to decide whether or not it is sung on the same pitch. To cover all the possibilities

Figure 42. Listing and Categorization of Breath Accents

1. Same Pitch—Same Vowel
a. Breath Accents Following Meaningful Syllables

Version Location	1A	3C	6C	2Ba	2Bb	7B	4D	5E	8Fa	8Fb	8Fc
A.2.e	2	2	2	0	0	2	2	2	4	4	0
B.2.c	1	0	0	0	0	0	0	0	0	0	0
C.1.c	0	0	0	0	0	0	1	0	0	0	0
D.2.a	2	2	2	2	2	2	2	0	2	2	0
E.2.a	2	2	2	2	2	2	2	0	1	2	0
I.1.c	1	0	0	0	0	0	0	0	0	0	0
I.5.a	0	1	0	0	0	0	1	0	0	0	0
R.1.e	1	1	1	0	1	1	1	0	0	1	0
S.3.a	0	0	0	0	0	0	0	0	0	1	0
T.1.e	1	0	0	0	1	1	1	0	0	1	0
U.4.d	1	0	0	0	0	1	1	0	0	1	0
W.1.b	0	0	0	0	0	0	0	0	0	1	0
X.3.a	1	0	0	0	1	1	1	0	0	0	0
Y.1.c	1	1	1	0	1	1	1	0	0	1	0

b. Breath Accents Following Breath Accents

Version Location	1A	3C	6C	2Ba	2Bb	7B	4D	5E	8Fa	8Fb	8Fc
A.2.e	1	1	1	1	1	1	1	1	2	2	0
D.2.a	1	1	1	1	1	1	1	0	1	1	0
E.2.a	1	1	1	1	1	1	1	0	0	1	0
G.2.b	0	0	0	0	0	0	0	0	1	1	0
J.1.a	1	1	1	0	1	1	1	0	0	0	0
W.1.b	0	0	0	0	0	0	0	0	0	1	0
W.1.b	1	1	1	0	0	1	0	0	0	0	0
X.3.c	0	0	0	0	0	0	0	0	0	0	1

2. Same Pitch—Different Vowel
a. Breath Accents Following Meaningful Syllable

Version Location	1A	3C	6C	2Ba	2Bb	7B	4D	5E	8Fa	8Fb	8Fc
A.2.e	0	0	0	2	2	0	0	0	0	0	0
T.1.e	0	1	1	0	0	0	0	0	0	0	0
U.4.d	0	1	1	0	1	0	0	0	0	0	0

3. Different Pitch—Same Vowel
a. Breath Accents Following Meaningful Syllable

Version Location	1A	3C	6C	2Ba	2Bb	7B	4D	5E	8Fa	8Fb	8Fc
A.2.d	1	1	1	0	0	0	0	0	0	0	0
B.2.c	0	0	0	1	1	1	0	0	0	1	0
C.1.c	1	1	1	1	1	1	0	0	1	1	0
D.2.b	0	0	1	0	0	0	0	0	1	1	0
F.2.b	1	0	0	1	1	1	0	0	0	1	0
J.1.a	2	2	2	0	2	2	2	0	0	0	0
K.1.c	1	1	1	0	1	1	1	0	0	0	0
M.2.c	1	1	1	0	1	1	0	0	0	1	0
O.1.c	1	1	1	0	1	1	0	0	0	1	0
S.3.b	0	0	0	0	1	1	0	0	0	0	0
W.1.b	1	1	1	0	1	1	1	0	0	1	0
X.3.a	0	1	1	0	0	0	0	0	0	0	0
x.3.b	1	1	1	0	1	1	1	0	0	1	0

Figure 42. *(Continued)*

b. Breath Accents Following Breath Accents

W.1.b	1	1	1	0	1	1	1	0	0	0	0
W.1.b	0	0	0	0	1	0	0	0	0	0	0
W.1.b	0	0	0	0	0	0	1	0	0	0	0
W.1.b	0	0	0	0	0	0	0	0	0	1	0
W.1.b	1	1	1	0	1	1	0	0	0	1	0
W.1.b	0	0	0	0	1	0	0	0	0	1	0
W.1.b	0	0	0	0	0	0	0	0	0	1	0
Z.3.c	1	1	1	0	1	1	1	0	0	1	1
Z.3.c	0	0	0	0	0	0	0	0	0	1	1

4. Different Pitch—Different Vowel
a. Breath Accents Following Meaningful Syllable

Version Location	1A	3C	6C	2Ba	2Bb	7B	4D	5E	8Fa	8Fb	8Fc
A.2.b	1	0	0	0	0	0	0	0	0	0	0
F.2.b	1	1	0	0	0	0	0	0	0	0	0

SUMMARY OF TOTALS

1. Same Pitch—Same Vowel
a. Breath Accents Following Meaningful Syllable

1st Mesa	3rd Mesa	Total
68	21	89

b. Breath Accents Following Breath Accents

1st Mesa	3rd Mesa	Total
32	11	43

2. Same Pitch—Different Vowel
a. Breath Accents Following Meaningful Syllable

1st Mesa	3rd Mesa	Total
9	0	9

3. Different Pitch—Same Vowel
a. Breath Accents Following Meaningful Syllable

1st Mesa	3rd Mesa	Total
62	9	71

b. Breath Accents Following Breath Accents

1st Mesa	3rd Mesa	Total
21	7	28

4. Different Pitch—Different Vowel
a. Breath Accents Following Meaningful Syllable

1st Mesa	3rd Mesa	Total
3	0	3

one would have to develop a half-dozen different categories. I prefer to simplify the matter since my principal interest is in discovering whether or not the following breath accent gives the impression of being sung on the same pitch as the syllable i follows. Thus I define "being sung on the same pitch" as follows: 1) the breath accent begins on the same pitch at which the previously sung syllable concludes and 2) the breath accent remains on that pitch. If any other situation pertains, the breath accent is not sung on "the same pitch." It will not be considered to be sung "on the same pitch" if 1) after beginning on the same pitch at which the preceding syllable concludes it moves to a different pitch, or 2) it begins on a different pitch than the concluding pitch of the preceding syllable.

These two characteristics, similarity or difference in vowel and similarity or difference in pitch, have been employed to divide breath accents into four categories (Fig. 42). Under categories 1a through 4a are listed breath accents which follow meaningful syllables. In categories 1b through 4b are listed those which follow other breath accents. The definitions made above concerning similarity or difference in vowel or pitch for breath accents following meaningful syllables apply equally to breath accents which follow other breath accents.

Most transcribers have reproduced the breath accent by means of two or more dots placed above or below a note sung to a particular syllable. The second and any subsequent dots refer to pulsations of the diaphragm. Thus the breath accent is conceived to be an extension of the same vowel sung on the same pitch. In transcribing the Hopi kachina dance song, I have found it necessary to expand this concept considerably (see Fig. 42). In preparing Figure 42 I did not consider the consonants commonly introduced before and after the repeated vowel. These will be discussed later.

The first phenomenon to be noted is that the majority of the breath accents, whether following the initial syllable or another breath accent, are sung on the same vowel. Thus for the First Mesa there are 58 breath accents which fall in class 1a, breath accent following syllable on same pitch and same vowel, and 62 breath accents in class 3a, following a syllable and differing in pitch but not in vowel, making a total of 130.

On the other hand, for the First Mesa there are only nine breath accents in class 2a, following syllable with same pitch but different vowel and three in class 4a, following syllable with different pitch and different vowel, a total of 12. Thus in the First Mesa

performances 91 percent of the breath accents following syllables are sung on the same vowel.

The preponderance of use of the same vowel is even more striking when those accents which follow other breath accents are considered. For the First Mesa there are 32 in class 1b, following breath accent with same pitch and same vowel and 21 in class 3b, following breath accent with different pitch but same vowel, a total of 53. There are no examples for the First Mesa of breath accents in classes 2b or 4b. Therefore the same vowel is utilized in 100 percent of all breath accents which follow other breath accents. Combining the two types of breath accents, classes a and b, for First Mesa we have a total of 183 in which the same vowel is sung and 12 in which it is not. Thus in the First Mesa performances the breath accent following the syllable or following another breath accent employs the same vowel 93 percent of the time.

In performances by the Third Mesa singer there are 21 breath accents in class 1a and 9 in 3a, a total of 30. There are none in classes 2a and 4a. Thus 100 percent are sung on the same vowel. In class 1b the Third Mesa singer performs 11 breath accents and seven in class 3b, a total of 18. Again, there are no examples of breath accents in classes 2b or 4b. Thus the same vowel is again sung 100 percent of the time. Combining breath accents sung after syllables and those sung after other breath accents yields is a total of 48 cases in which the same vowel is sung and none in which it is not. The Third Mesa singer therefore sings the same vowel in all breath accents or in 100 percent of the cases.

Combining First Mesa and Third Mesa practice, we find that the same vowel is sung in 231 cases and a different vowel in 12 cases. The same vowel is therefore employed in 95 percent of all breath accents sung.

The percentages of breath accents sung on the same pitch as the previous syllable or breath accent are not nearly as large as those involving the same vowel. In class A the First Mesa singers sing 77 breath accents on the same pitch as the preceding syllable and 65 on a different pitch. The percentage sung on the same pitch is therefore 54 percent. In class B, breath accents following breath accents, the First Mesa singers sing 32 on the same pitch and 21 on a different pitch, the percentage on the same pitch being 61 percent. Combining the figures for the two types of breath accents, we have 109 sung on the same pitch and 86 sung on a different pitch, 55 percent then on the same pitch.

Following the same procedure for the Third Mesa

Figure 43. Consonants Employed in Breath Accents

	-	y-	-y	y-y	l-	l-l	l-y
1st Mesa	23	34	26	67	11	2	4
3rd Mesa	14	7	6	13	1	0	0
TOTALS	37	41	32	80	12	2	4

singer, we find in class A 21 breath accents sung on the same pitch and nine on a different pitch. Thus 70 percent are sung on the same pitch. In class B the Third Mesa singer performs 11 breath accents on the same pitch and seven on a different pitch. The percentage of those sung on the same pitch is 61 percent. Combining figures for the Third Mesa we have 32 breath accents sung on the same pitch and 16 sung on a different pitch, the percentage of those sung on the same pitch being 66.

When the figures for First Mesa and Third mesa are combined, we have a total of 141 sung on the same pitch, 102 on a different pitch. Thus 58 percent of the breath accents are sung on the same pitch, compared with 95 percent sung on the same vowel.

It should be noted that when breath accents are not sung on the same pitch as the previous syllable they are usually sung at a lower pitch or descend to this lower pitch. When in rare cases they are sung on a higher pitch or ascend, it is usually within a melisma like that seen in segment W.

In Figure 43 I list the consonants and combinations of consonants which is employed with the breath accents. In some cases none is employed, that is, the breath accent consists of a vowel only. The vowels are indicated by hyphens. A hyphen can, of course, represent any vowel.

The most common form taken by the breath accent is a vowel both preceded and followed by the glide y. Next in number of occurrences is the vowel preceded by y. There are a larger number of breath accents consisting of a vowel only than there are of a vowel followed by a y. The Third Mesa singer makes proportionately greater use of this form of the breath accent than the First Mesa singers.

The consonant l is used much less frequently than the y. It either precedes the vowel, precedes and follows the vowel, or precedes the vowel which is then followed by a y. There are no cases where the vowel is not preceded but is followed by an l. The Third Mesa singer makes use of the l in only one breath accent.

There are 37 cases in which the breath accent consists of a vowel only and 171 in which one or more consonants are added. Therefore consonants are added 82 percent of the time.

Thus only two consonants are employed in singing breath accents, the glide y and the l, the former predominating. If we count each individual occurrence of a consonant (thus y-y is counted as two instances of y), y is present 157 times and l 18, the former thus occurring 89 percent of the time.

3.10.3b. Non-symbolic Vocables

According to the informants, most of the vocables were meaningless but some, along with the melody to which they were sung, symbolized the kachina being represented. In Figure 44 the vocables found within in the song, that is, not in the Moccasin nor the Identificatory Introduction, are reproduced. These all occur in the first half of that part of the song which was transcribed. The singers from the First Mesa and the one from the Third Mesa sing *taawanawita* in different places, so all the singers do not necessarily sing the vocables in the same place. For this reason they have been divided into three sections. In a. are given the vocables sung by the First Mesa singers in Segment G. In b. are those sung in two performances by the Third Mesa singer in Segment J and the first few syllables of Segment K. In c. are the vocables sung by all singers jointly (beginning with the fifth syllable in the segment sung by the First Mesa singers) through the last syllable of Segment L, the end of the first section of the song. Note that the singers do not necessarily sing the same number of syllables in b. and c. Where a syllable is given for some performances but none for others two factors may apply. There may be a rest instead of a syllable or, more frequently, the performer moves immediately to the next syllable. This will be further explained as we examine b.

In Segment G the singers from the First Mesa show considerable agreement in the syllables sung. The five syllables in performances 1A, 2Ba, 2Bb, and 7B are identical. Although they are different from those sung by singers A and B, those in performances 3C and 6C match each other throughout. Performance 4D is the least consistent. In syllables 1 and 2 he is in agreement with singers A and B and in his fourth and fifth syllables with singer C. However, his third syllable is not consistent with that sung by any other singer.

Figure 44. Comparison of Vocables

a.

Performance	Segment				
	G.2				
1A	hay	yay	hay	yay	yaw
3C	ha	la	ho	o	o
6C	ha	la	ho	o	o
2Ba	hay	yay	hay	yay	yaw
2Bb	hay	yay	hay	yay	yaw
7B	hay	yay	hay	yay	yaw
4D	hay	yay	wo	o	o

b.

Performance	Segment				K		
	J						
8Fa	hey	ye	hey	hæy	hey	hæy	
8Fb	lay	yay			hey	yey	yey

c.

Performance	Segment					L				
	K									
1A		hi	li	yi		he	yay	ta	ta	ta
3C	ley	yey	hey	yey	yey	hi	yey	na	yəm	
6C	leh	yey	hey	yey	ye	hi	hey	na	əm	
2Ba	ney		hey	yey	yey	ey	hey	tay	əm	
2Bb	ley		ey	yey	yey	ey	hey	ta	m	
7B	ley	yey	ey	yey	yey	ey	hey	la	m	
4D	ley	yey	hey	m	m	ey	hay	tay	yey	yay
8Fa	hæy					ey	hey	la	m	
8Fb	hay	hey				la	le	m		

In b. singer F does not sing the same number of syllables in his two performances. The three syllables sung in 8Fb in Segment K are followed by a rest. The other gaps are caused by the necessity of matching all performances by segments. They do not represent a hiatus in the singing; the singer goes on immediately to the next syllable. The only agreement between the two performances is found in the first syllable of K, *hey*.

The situation in c. is somewhat complex. There is a maximum of five syllables in the remainder of segment K (that part in which vocables are sung) and a similar maximum of five syllables in segment L. Again, in segment K the Third Mesa singer does not sing as many syllables as those in performances by the First Mesa singers. 8Fa has one syllable which is followed by a rest; 8Fb has two syllables. Both then move immediately to the first syllable of segment L.

Performance 1A begins with what my second translator described as a meaningful Zuni word, *liiλa*. Under the first syllable of this word, *lii*, the syllable *ley* is sung by in 3C, 6C, 2Bb, 7B, and 4D. Only the syllable sung in 2Ba differs. Under the second syllable sung in 1A, all First Mesa singers but B in 2Ba and 2Bb sing *yey*. The latter have rests at this point. The two syllables sung in 8Fa and 8Fb

while 1A has *liiλa* do not match any of those sung by the First Mesa singers nor do they match each other. None of the remaining First Mesa singers is in agreement with the third, fourth, or fifth syllables sung in 1A. However, the other singers are at least in partial agreement. For the third syllable, four sing *hey* and two *ey*. For the fourth syllable, five First Mesa singers sing *yey* and one, D, sings *m*. For the fifth and last syllable of segment K, four of the First Mesa singers sing *yey*, one *ye*, and one *m*. This is the first time in this figure that the two performances by singer C have not matched. 3C has *yey* and 6C *ye*.

In segment L some singers perform five syllables and some four. 8Fb is an exception since it contains only three syllables in this segment. For the first syllable, four First Mesa singers sing *ey* as does F in 8Fa, the first time that there is a match between a performance by the Third Mesa singer and those of the First Mesa singers. In addition, two First Mesa singers sing *hi*. 8Fb does not match either 8Fa nor any of the syllables sung by the First Mesa singers. For the second syllable of segment L there are four performances by First Mesa singers and one by the Third Mesa singer of *hey* and two by First Mesa singers of *yey*. Again, the two performances by the Third Mesa singer are not in agreement. For the third

Figure 45. Ratios of Agreement in Figure 44

a.

SEGMENT G

1	2	3	4	5
hay-5/7	yay-5/7	hay-4/7	yay-4/7	yaw-4/7
ha-2/7	la-2/7	ho-2/7	o-3/7	o-3/7
		wo-1/7		

b.

SEGMENT J			K.1			
1	2	3	4	5	6	7
-0/2	-0/2	hey-1/1	hæy-1/1	hey-2/2	-0/2	yey-1/1

c.

SEGMENT K.2					L				
1	2	3	4	5	6	7	8	9	10
ley-5/8	yey-4/5	hey-4/7	yey-5/7	yey-4/7	ey-4/7	hey-4/7	ta-2/7	əm-2/7	ta-1/2
ney-1/8	hey-1/5	ey-2/7	li-1/7	yi-2/7	hi-2/7	yay-1/7	na-2/7	m-2/7	yay-1/2
hæy-1/8		hi-1/7	m-1/7	ye-1/7	he-1/7		tay-2/7	ta-1/7	yəm-1/7
hay-1/8				m-1/7				la-1/7	yey-1/7

syllable of segment L, two performances by First Mesa singers are *ta*, two have *na*, and two have *tay*. One has *la* with a matching syllable by 8Fa. 8Fb is not in agreement with any of the others. Finally, I come to the fourth syllable of segment L. Two performances by a First Mesa singer are *əm* and two plus a performance in 8Fa are *m*. There are no other agreements.

The above exposition of agreement or non-agreement in syllables sung by singers of First and Third Mesas is made explicit in tabular form in Figure 45. The syllables found in a., b., and c., respectively,

are numbered. There are five such syllables in a., seven in b., and ten in c. A number is given if at least one singer is uttering the syllable at this point.

In the figure the upper line or rank of fractions found under the numbers represents the largest ratio of agreement seen of the particular syllable. The left number of the fractions represents those performances which are in agreement as to the the syllable sung; that to the right of the slash represents the number of singers performing at this point. Thus 5/7 indicates that there are seven performances and that five singers sing the same syllable while the other

Figure 46. Comparison of Vocables Found in the Moccasin

PERF.	GROUP I						GROUP II					
1A	ha	ya	hu	hu	ya	vaɣ	ha	ya	hay	hay	ay	ey
3C	ha	ha	həl	həl	a	we	a	ha	ha	ha	lal	
6C	ha	lə	ha	lə	hal	la	ley	hal	a	ha	lal	
2Bb	a	ha	a	hal	al		a	ha	al	ha	la	
7B	a	ha	lal	hal	lal	ley	a	ha	al	hal	lal	le
4D	a	ha	a	ha	lal	la	ey	hey	yey	hey	yey	le	le
8Fb	aw	aw	haw	yaw	yə		a	ha	haw	a	yaw	ya
8Fc	haw	aw	haw	yaw	ya	ey	aw	a	haw	aw	ay	

PERF.	GROUP III							GROUP IV						
1A	hey	ey	hey	hey	ay	ey		hey	ey	hey	ey	
3C	hey	ey	ey	hey	ey	ey		hey	æ	hey	æ	
6C	hey	e	hey	hey	æ	yæ		hey	æ	hey	æ	
2Bb	ey	ey	hey	ey	e	y		hey	æ	hey	æ	
7B	i	hi	hey	hey	yey	yey		hey	ye	hey	y	
4C	a	ha	a	hal	la	la	lay lay	la	la	lay	
8Fb	hey	yə	hey	yə	hey	yə		ha	hey	ye	hey	ym
8Fc	hey	ey	ey	hey	æ	ye	æ	hey	ey	ya	he	ey	ya	he	ey	ya

Figure 47. Ratios of Agreement of Vocables in Figure 46

GROUP I

1	2	3	4	5	6	7
ha-3/8	ha-4/8	a-2/8	hal-2/8	ya-2/8	ley-1/1	ley-1/1
a-3/8	aw-2/8	haw-2/8	yaw-2/8	lal-2/8	we-1/6	
aw-1/8	lə-1/8	hu-1/8	hu-1/8	a-1/8	ley-1/6	
haw-1/8	ya-1/8	həl-1/8	həl-1/8	hal-1/8	vay-1/6	
		ha-1/8	lə-1/8	al-1/8	ey 1/6	
		lal-1/8	ha-1/8	yə-1/8		

GROUP II

1	2	3	4	5	6	7
a-4/8	ha-2/8	ha-2/8	ha-2/8	lal-2/7	lə-2/4	l-1/1
ha-1/8	l-2/8	al-2/8	hay-1/8	ay-2/7	ey-1/4	
hal-1/8	ya-1/8	haw-2/8	lal-1/8	la-1/7	ya-1/4	
ey-1/8	hey-1/8	hay-1/8	hal-1/8	yey-1/7		
aw-1/8		yey-1/8	hey-1/8	yaw-1/7		
			a-1/8			
			aw-1/8			

GROUP III

1	2	3	4	5	6	7	8
hey-5/8	ey-4/8	hey-4/8	hey-5/8	æ-2/8	ey-2/8	lay-1/2	lay-1/2
ey-1/8	e-1/8	ey-2/8	ey-1/8	ay-1/8	yə-2/8	æ-1/2	
i-1/8	hi-1/8	yey-1/8	hal-1/8	ey-1/8	yæ-1/8		
a-1/8	ha-1/8	a-1/8	yə-1/8	e-1/8	yey-1/8		
	yə-1/8			yey-1/8	la-1/8		
				la-1/8	ye-1/8		
				hey-1/8			

GROUP IV

1	2	3	4	5	6	7	8	9
hey-5/8	æ-3/8	hey-5/8	æ-3/7	ym-1/2	ya-1/1	he-1/1	ey-1/1	ya-1/1
la-1/8	ey-2/8	lay-1/8	ey-1/7	ey-1/2				
ha-1/8	ye-1/8	ye-1/8	yə-1/7					
he-1/8	la-1/8	ya-1/8	hey-1/7					
	hey-1/8		he-1/7					

two do not. The ratio 0/2 indicates that there are two singers performing at this point and that they are not in agreement. The ratio 1/1 indicates that only one singer is performing. He, of course, is in agreement with himself. The fractions or ratios offered are given in ranks from one to five, in descending order of agreement.

It will be noted above that in a. there is a majority of agreement in each case, 5/7 or 4/7. In b. there is only one point where the two performances are in agreement, the fifth syllable, which is marked 2/2. In c. there is a majority agreement in seven out of ten cases. In the tenth case only two singers are performing and the first and second ranks are equal, 1/1.

Figure 46 offers a comparison of the vocables sung in the Moccasin. Note that it is organized in four groups. It should be remembered that singer D sang seven groups in the Moccasin rather than four. His first two groups matched those of the others, but his sixth and seventh groups have been matched with the third and fourth groups of the other singers. Consideration of his third and fourth groups has been omitted (see 3.7).

Figure 47 is an analysis of the ratios of agreement found in Figure 46. It is organized in the same fashion as Figure 45. There is a maximum of seven syllables in each of the first two groups, eight in the third group, and nine in the fourth group.

There is considerably less agreement in the vocables sung by the various singers in the Moccasin than there is in the vocables in Figures 44-45. In a. of Figure 44, there is a majority of agreement among all First Mesa singers in all five syllables sung and in c. among all singers in seven out of ten syllables sung. However, in b. of Figure 44 only 8Fb and 8Fc are compared and there is little agreement. In the Moccasin, in which the beginning of each group is sung by all eight singers, there are, on the other hand, only four cases where the ratio represents the majority of the performances, 5/8. This occurs in groups 3

Example 1   Example 2

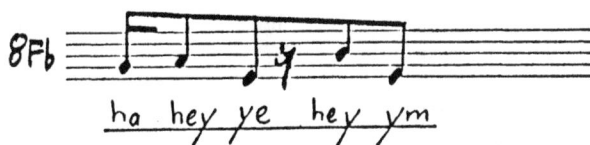

and 4. Omitting occurrences of 1/1, which represent only one singer, there are, in addition, five cases in which half of the singers agree, 4/8. These are found in groups 1-3, but not in 4.

From the point of view of the Hopi there may be more agreement than this analysis indicates. In the first place, since all singers do not sing the same number of syllables, there is no means of determining exactly which syllable should be matched with which. All that can be done is to match the syllables in the sequence in which they are sung, that is, the first syllable sung by all singers, then the second syllable sung by all singers, etc. As singers fall out, only the syllables sung by those who remain can be

matched. Since all singers do not sing the same number of syllables in a particular group, the denominator of the fraction diminishes toward the end of the group and the ratios produced are of less and less significance. If there were a customary number of syllables to be sung, there is no way I can determine which singer may have added a syllable or which may have omitted one.

In the second place, I have transcribed the vowels in the vocables as I heard them. However, in the Hopi phonetic system there is no ə and no æ. Thus as the *ey* when sung may represent *i* as spoken, the ə or æ may represent to the Hopi ear merely a modification of one of their standard vowels, *e* or *a*.

Figure 48. Ratios of Possible Symbolic Vocables in Group 4 of the Moccasin

A	B	C	D
hey-6/7	æ-3/7	hey-6/7	æ-3/7
ey-1/7	ye-2/7	he-1/7	ey-2/7
	ey-1/7		yə-1/7
	ya-1/7		ym-1/7

3.10.3c. Symbolic Vocables

I was told by a number of informants that what was sung at the beginning of a kachina dance song symbolizes the kachina represented at the dance and by two informants that what was sung at the end of the song also represents the kachina performing. It is only in the latter part of group 4 of the Moccasin that I find much similarity in the performances. I therefore consider the last four pitches as sung by the First Mesa singers, consisting of two descending melodic intervals of a fourth or fifth and the four syllables to which they are sung to possibly represent the phenomenon reported by my informants. Since the various singers sing different numbers of syllables in group 4, these patterns are not matched in Figure 47. They have been matched in Figure 48 where the four syllables are indicated by letters A, B, C, and D. In all performances by First Mesa singers except D these syllables are sung to two descending intervals of a fourth or fifth. This is shown in Example 1 above.

In 8Fb singer F precedes the first note of this descending interval by a note a second below but omits it the second time the interval is performed. In 8Fc, on the other hand, singer F performs the interval three times, each time with the additional preceding note. These are seen above.

In Figure 48 the initial syllables sung preceding the descending interval of singer F (see Example 2 above) are omitted from consideration. As singer D in 4D does not perform the two descending intervals

at the end of the fourth group of the Moccasin, his performance is omitted from consideration in Figure 48 and thus only seven performances are included in the ratios. It will be seen that six of seven performances of syllable A are *hey* and the seventh is *ey*. A similar consistency is found in the performance of syllable C. Six of seven are *hey* and one is *he*.

No such consistency is found in the syllables sung to the lower pitches of the interval, syllables B and D. In syllable B three performances are of *æ* and two are of *ye*. The situation is similar in syllable D where there are three performances of *æ* and two of *ey*. In all cases I have omitted consideration of a syllable when it is performed only once.

It would seem from the above that this particular kachina is typified by a descending interval of a fourth or fifth, the upper pitch of which is sung to *hey* (in *ey* the consonant preceding the vowel is missing, in *he* the consonant following the vowel) and the second or lower pitch sung to whatever syllable is convenient. Here, again, I have written the vowels *æ* and *ə*. Both could be considered modifications of standard Hopi vowels and therefore the ratios of agreement would be considerably larger.

Figure 49 offers a comparison of vocables found in the Identificatory Introduction. This symbolic introduction to the song consists of four groups.

The ratios derived from Figure 49 are given in Figure 50. Figure 50 is organized in the same manner as Figures 45 and 47.

Of the four groups forming the Identificatory Introduction Group 2 has four syllables and the remaining three have a maximum of five syllables. It should be remembered that not all singers include the Identificatory Introduction in their performance.

There is considerable agreement in the syllables sung. In the first three groups the last syllable is not sung by all five singers nor are the last two syllables of group 4. Omitting these five syllables from the total 19 sung, we have 14 by all five singers. Of these there is a majority agreement on the syllables sung in

Figure 49. Comparison of Vocables in the Identificatory Introduction

PERFORMANCE

1A	hu	yu	hey	yey		hey	yey	hey	yey	hey	yə		hay	yay		hey	yey	hey
3C	hu	yu	hey	ye	hay	hey	yey	hey	yey	hay	yæ	hay	ye	yay	hay	yey	he	ye	yey
6C	hu	yu	hey	ye	hay	hey	yey	hey	yey	hay	yæ	hey	ye	yay	hay	yey	he	ye	yey
4D	a	ha	ya	ya	hay	hey	yey	yey	hey	hey	yay	yay	hay		hey	yey	yey
8Fa	ha	ya	ya	ya		hey	yey	yey		haw	yaw	yaw	yaw		hey	hey	hey

8 cases of the 14. There are two cases of the ratio 5/5, one of 4/5, and five of 3/5. If those instances where fewer than five singers are heard are also counted, there is one case of 3/3, one of 3/4, and three of 2/2. When these are added there is a majority opinion in 13 of the 19 cases, or 68 percent.

Thus there is greater agreement among the singers in the vocables sung in the Identificatory Introduction than in those sung in the Moccasin or within the song. Again, this agreement might be enhanced if the ə or æ were taken to represent standard Hopi vowels. It is, of course, appropriate that there be more consistency in the vowels sung in the Identificatory Introduction than elsewhere. Without such consistency, the symbolic meaning of the vocables would not be effective. It is interesting to note that the percentage of agreement concerning the syllables sung in the Identificatory Introduction, 68 percent, is smaller than that found in its melodic contours, 85 percent. Since we are dealing with that section of the song which symbolizes the kachina dance songs, at least, variation in phones is more culturally acceptable.

Figure 50. Ratios of Agreement of Symbolic Vocables in the Identificatory Introduction

GROUP I

1	2	3	4	5
hu-3/5	yu-3/5	hey-3/5	ye-2/5	hay-3/3
a-1/5	ha-1/5	ya-2/5	ya-2/5	
ha-1/5	ya-1/5		yey-1/5	

GROUP II

1	2	3	4
hey-5/5	yey-5/5	hey-3/5	yey-3/4
		yey-2/5	hey-1/4

GROUP III

1	2	3	4	5
hey-2/5	yæ-2/5	hay-3/5	ye-2/5	yay-2/2
hay-2/5	yə-1/5	yay-1/5	yay-1/5	
haw-1/5	yay-1/5	yaw-1/5	hay-1/5	
	yaw-1/5	hey-1/5	yaw-1/5	

GROUP IV

1	2	3	4	5
hey-3/5	yey-4/5	hey-2/5	ye-2/2	yey-2/2
hay-2/5	hey-1/5	yey-1/5		
		he-2/5		

Chapter 4 The Lullaby

4.1. Singing the Child to Sleep

The "black beetle" or "stink bug" lullaby has been known throughout the Hopi Reservation at least since the beginning of this century. It is primarily sung by women, but also occasionally by men to their children. In the past it was the custom of Hopi women to strap their infants to cradleboards which they then tied to their backs to carry their infants from place to place while they worked. The child was sung to sleep while on the cradleboard or by either sex while being held in the arms. In the latter case the child's back was simultaneously rubbed. The lullaby has no pulse since no coordination of kinetic or musical rhythm is involved as there would be, for example, in rocking a child to sleep in a cradle.

4.2. Corpus of Recordings to be Studied

The analysis in this chapter is based on 11 recorded performances by six informants. A list of the recordings and the provenance of each is given in Figure 51, where the performers are represented by capital letters and the chronological sequence in which the recordings were made by numerals, as in Figure 13 (p. 23).

There is at least one recording from each Mesa area and the recordings span the period from ca. 1903 through 1960. Singer K was recorded on two different days for a total of four performances of the song. Singer H was a Navaho who sang Hopi songs (see 1.4).

4.3. The Spoken Texts and Translations

Figure 52 offers the text of the lullaby as it is spoken, not as sung, and its translation into English. The actual meaning of *puwva*, which in repetition forms the refrain, is "he falls asleep," or "he slept." "Go to sleep" is the English equivalent given me by the Hopi who acted as my translator for the lullabies. In the song an analogy is made between a Hopi carrying an infant on a cradleboard and the posture of indigenous beetles who are frequently seen one car-

Figure 51. Provenance of Lullaby Recordings

1G	Sung by a man from the village of Oraibi, Third Mesa. Recorded by Natalie Curtis, ca. 1903-1905.
2H	Sung by a man at Fort Wingate School. Recorded by Willard Rhodes, 1941. Library of Congress #AAFS L43.
3I	Sung by a man from Shipaulovi, Second Mesa. Recorded by Robert Black, 1956.
4J	Sung by a woman from Sichomovi, First Mesa. Recorded by George List at Polacca, Arizona, 2 August 1960.
5K	Sung by a woman from Sichomovi, First Mesa. Recorded by George List at Polacca, Arizona, 2 August 1960.
6K	Singer K, recorded by George List at Polacca, Arizona, 8 August 1960.
7K	Singer K, recorded by George List at Polacca, Arizona, 8 August 1960.
8K	Singer K, recorded by George List at Polacca, Arizona, 8 August 1960.
9L	Sung by a women from Sichomovi, First Mesa. Recorded by George List at Polacca, Arizona, 8 August 1960.
10L	Singer L, recorded by George List at Polacca, Arizona, 8 August 1960.
11L	Singer L, recorded by George List at Polacca, Arizona, 8 August 1960.

rying the other on his back. This beetle is known colloquially as "stink bug" since it produces a foul odor when crushed.

Figure 52. Spoken Text of the Lullaby

puwva	puwva (etc.)	hohoyaw'u	supööpave
Go to sleep!	Go to sleep!	Beetle	Right on the road
naa'iikwi'ukyang'u			puwva (etc.)
While carrying each other on the back			Go to sleep!

4.4. The Sung Performances

As indicated previously, performances of this lullaby display no easily discernible pulse. In this they are similar to Hopi announcement chants, neither being associated with a kinetic activity. The durational values found in the transcriptions were determined by establishing an artificial pulse an eighth note in value. This produced tempi ranging from MM 108 to MM 144. In Figure 53 I give a comparison of all 11 performances of the lullaby.

The comparative score offered in Figure 53 is similar to that given in Figure 15. The reader is

Figure 53. Comparative Score of Performances of the Lullaby

Figure 53. *(Continued)*

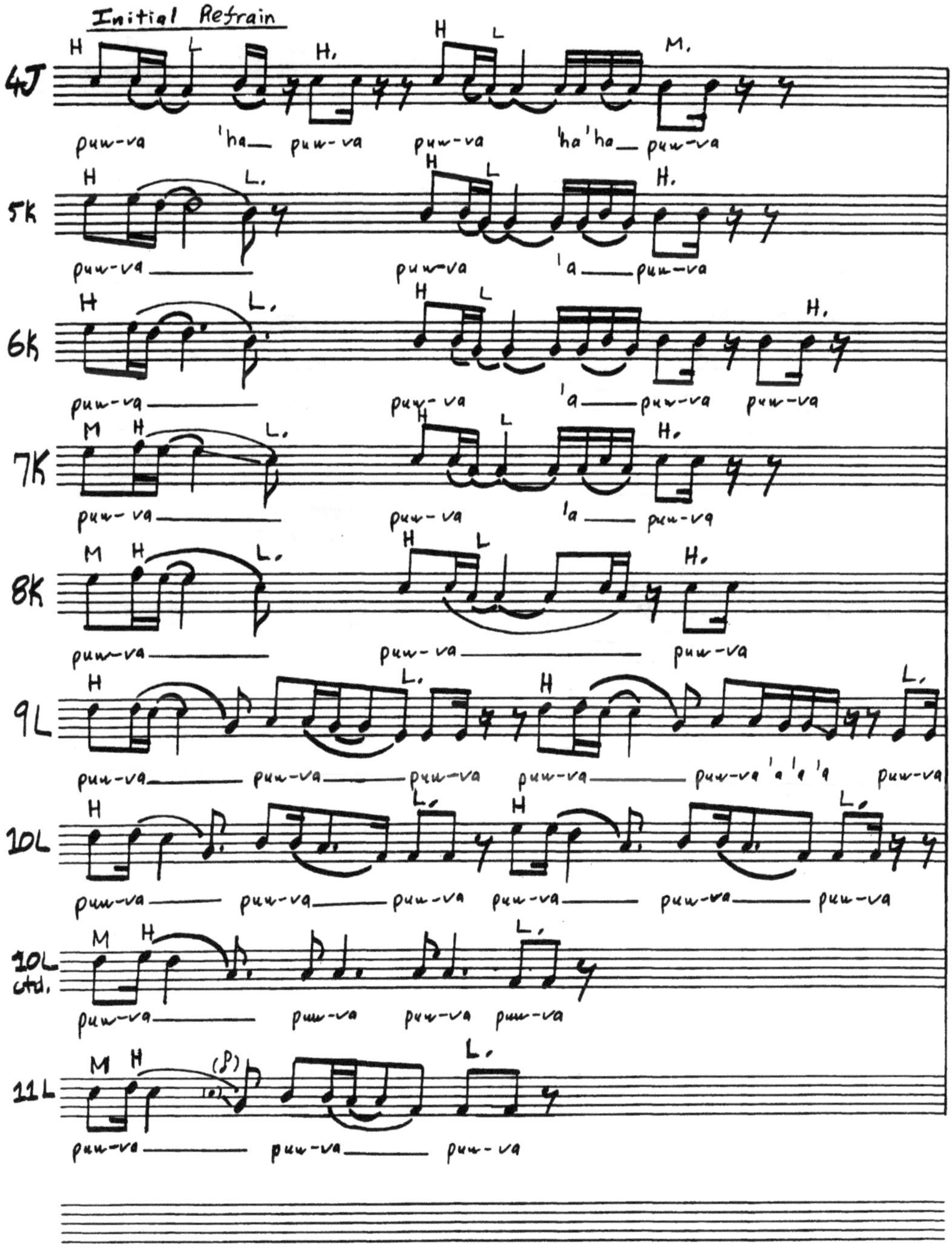

Figure 53. *(Continued)*

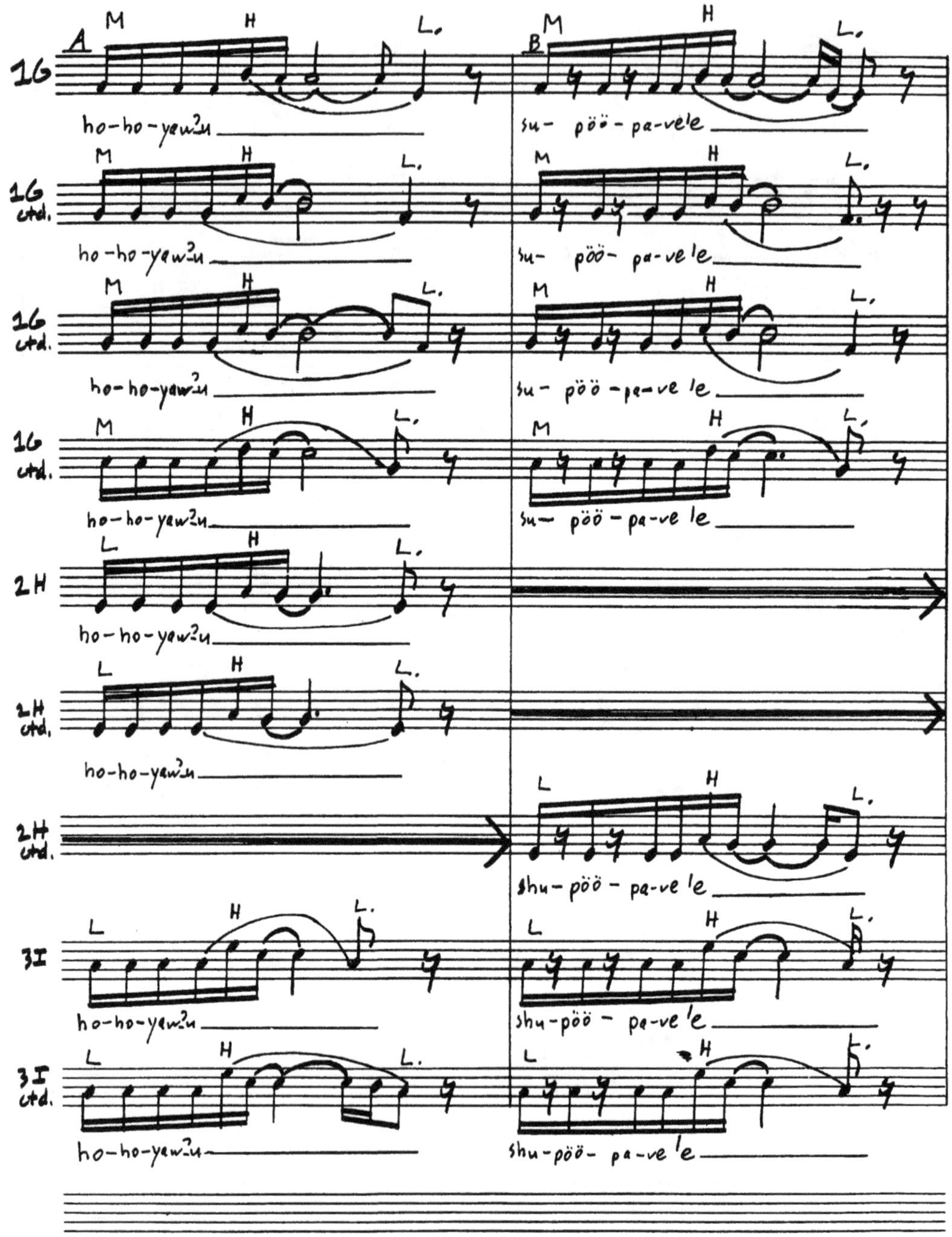

Figure 53. *(Continued)*

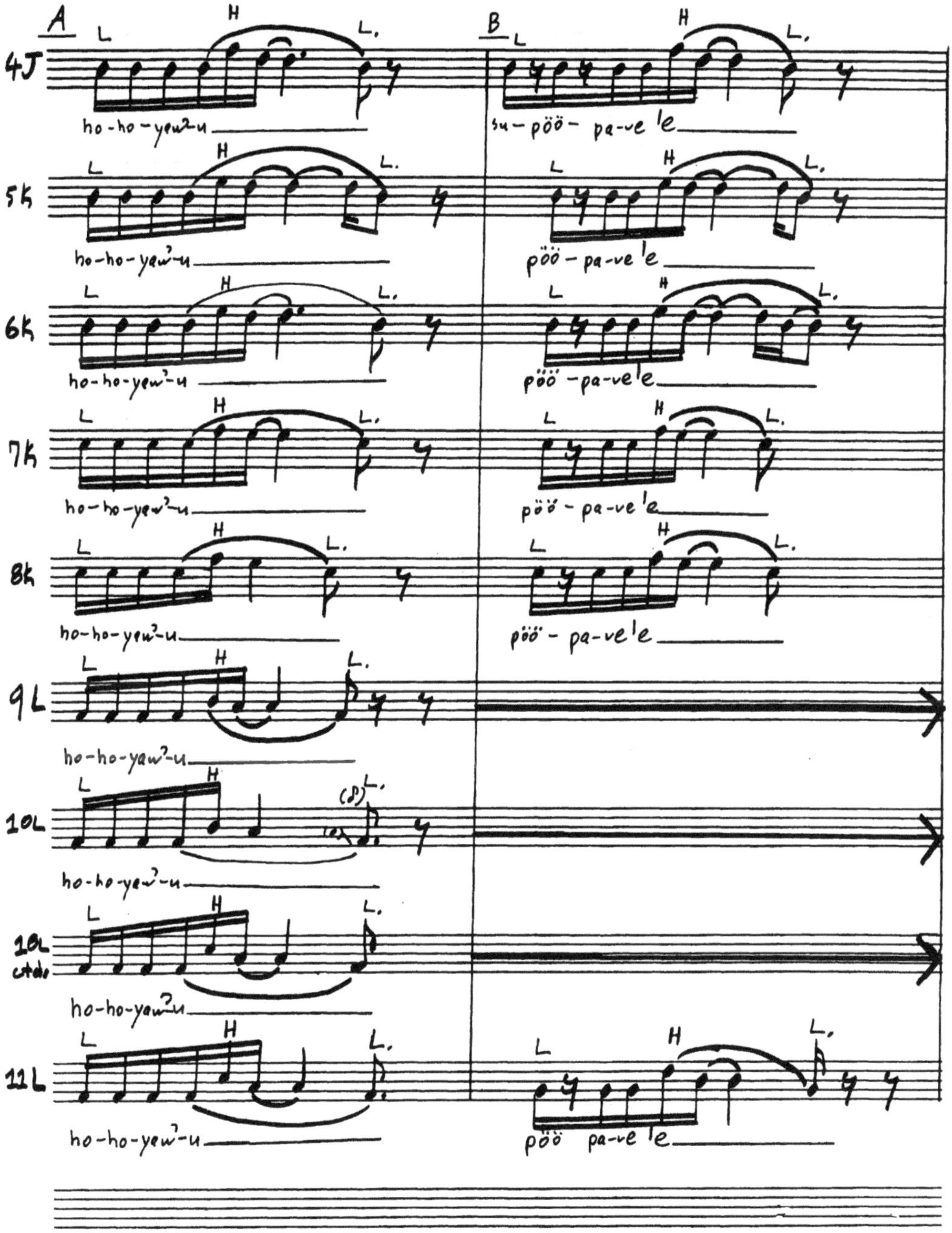

Figure 53. *(Continued)*

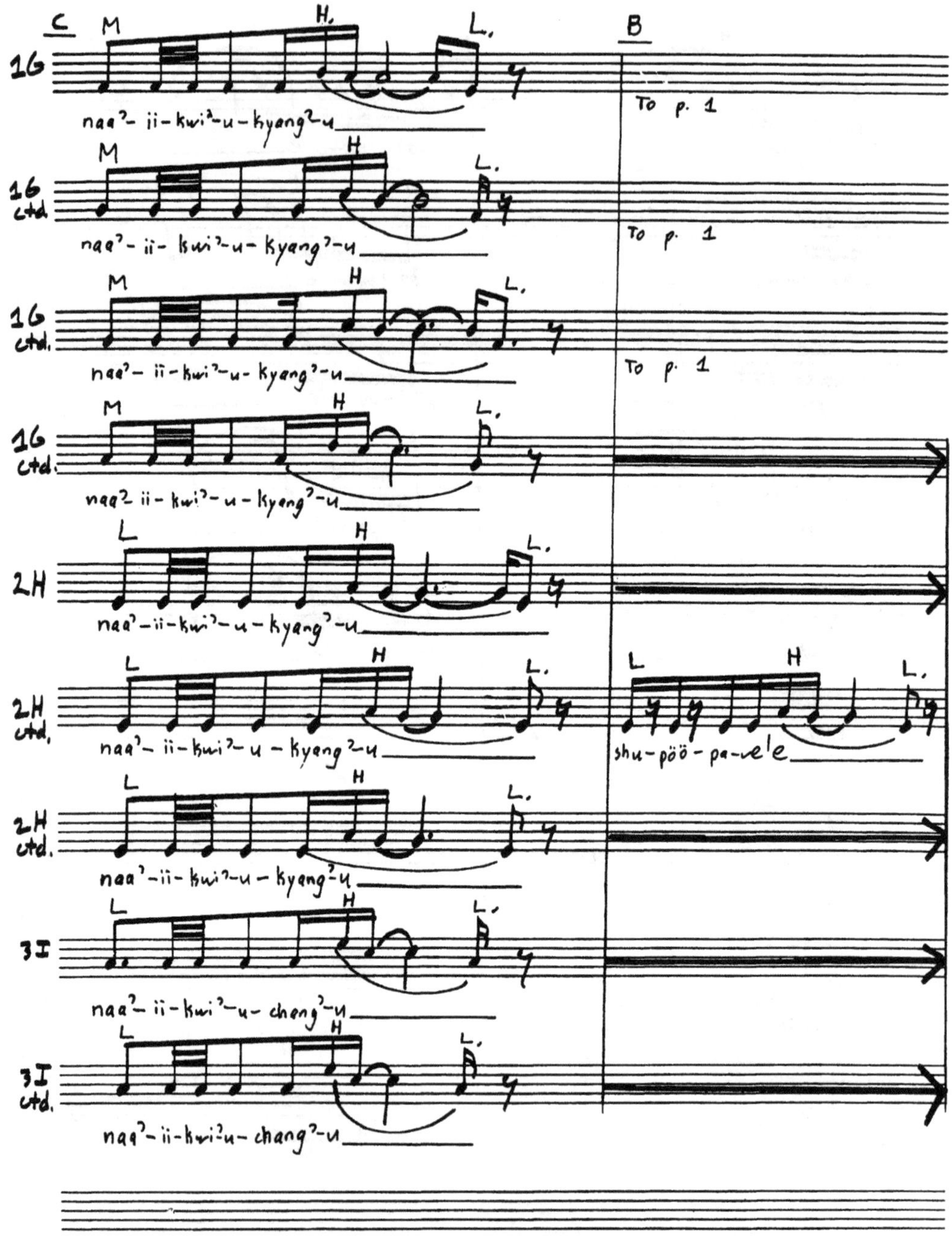

Figure 53. *(Continued)*

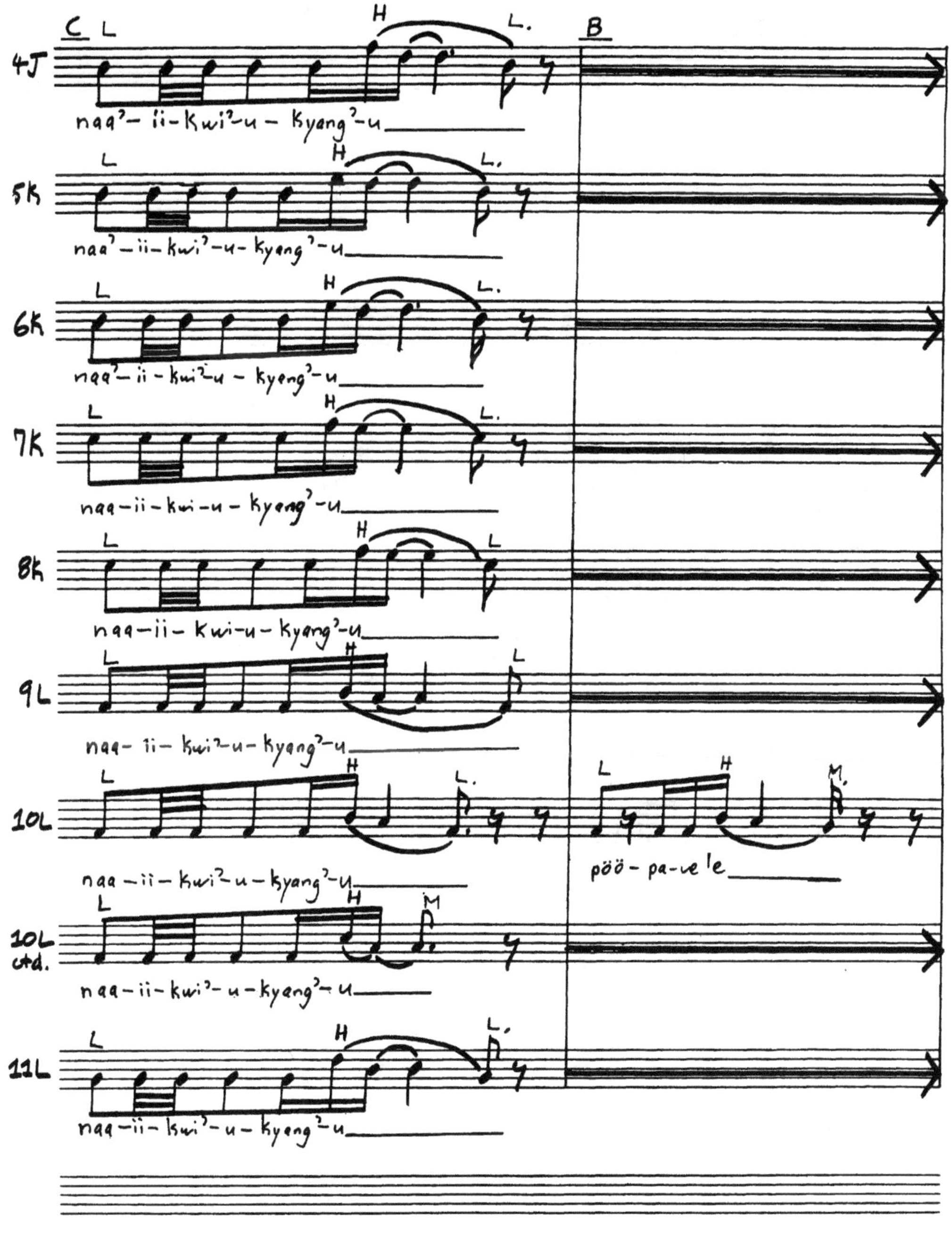

Figure 53. *(Continued)*

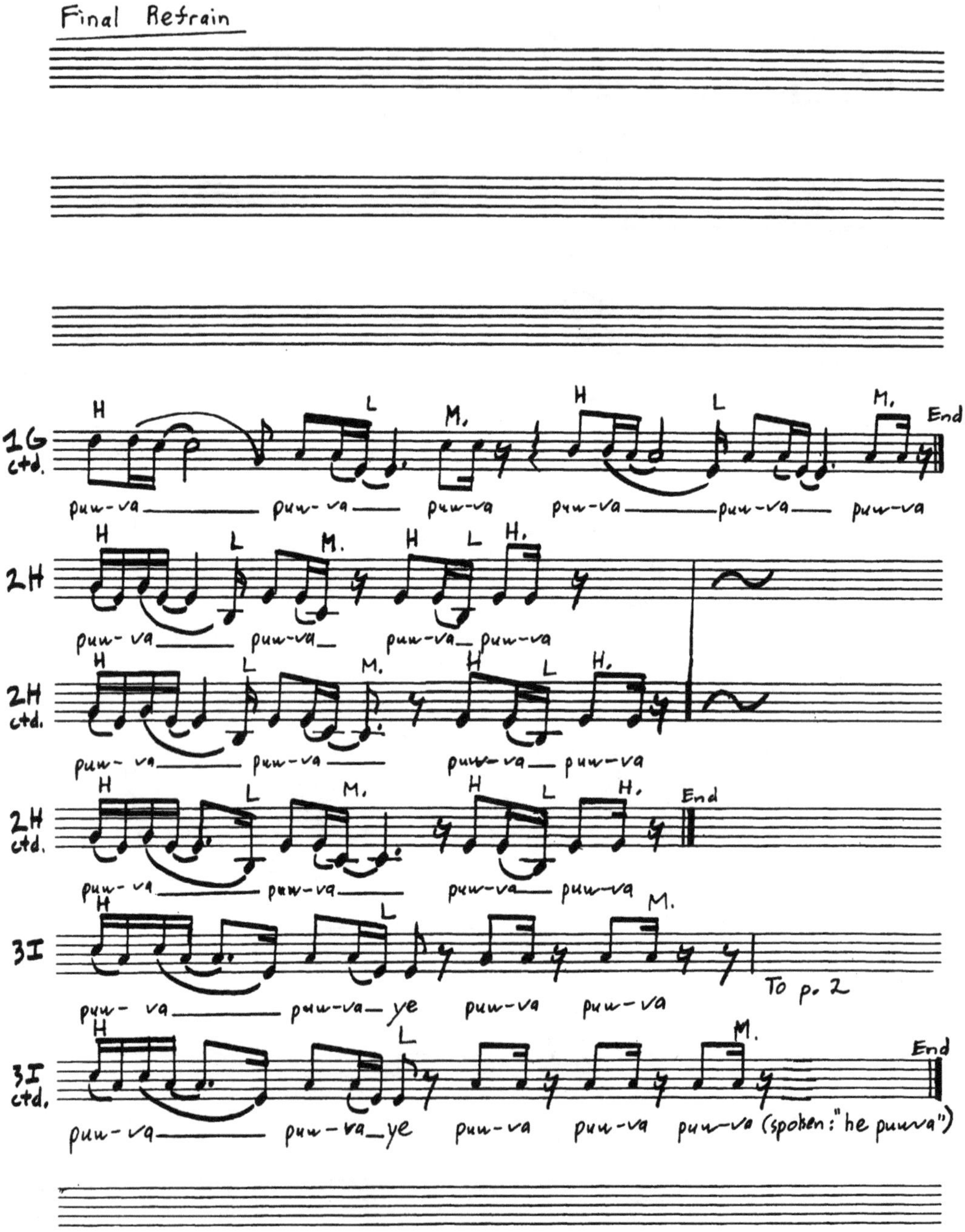

Figure 53. *(Continued)*

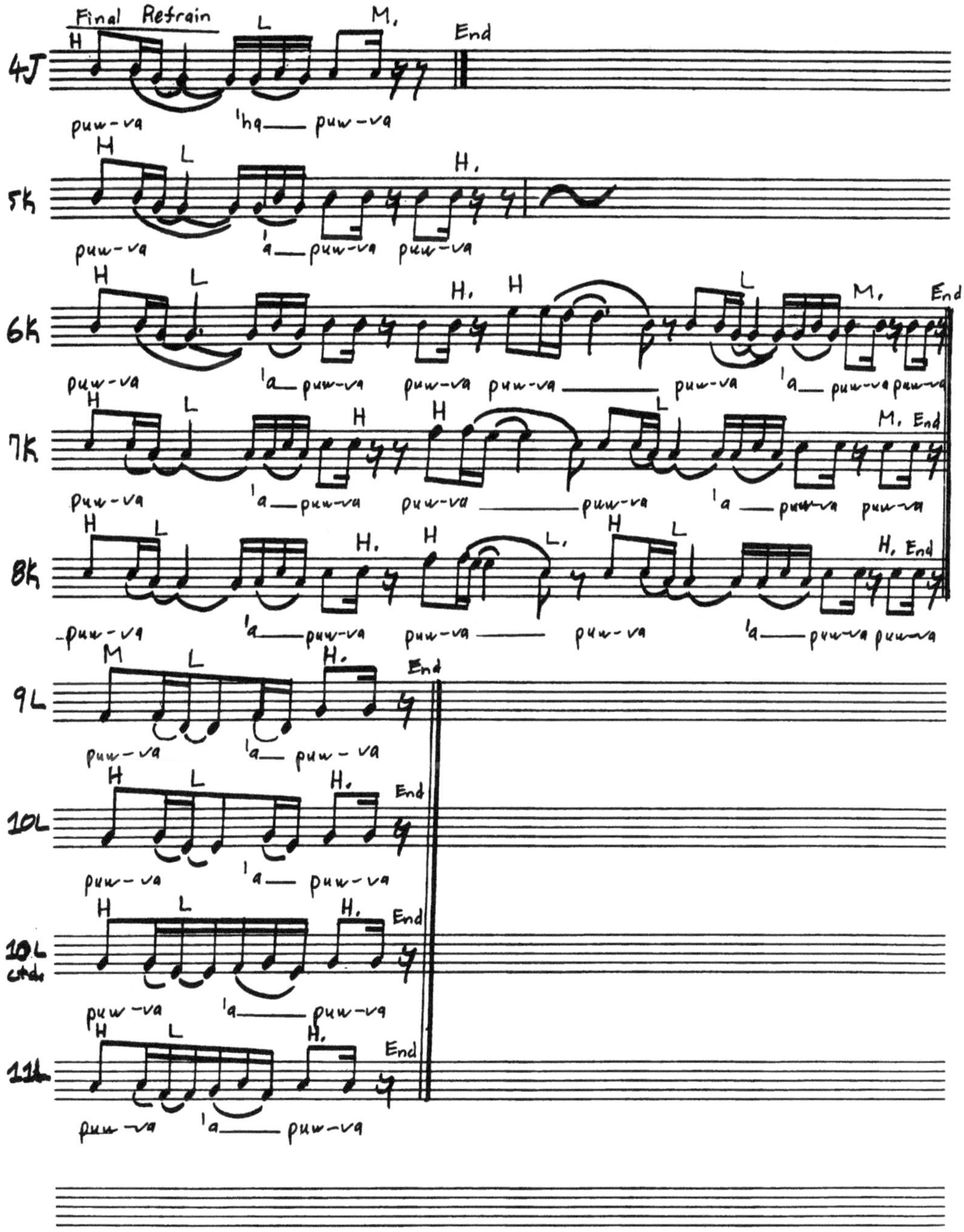

Figure 53. *(Continued)*

Figure 53. *(Continued)*

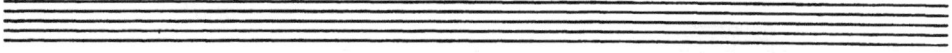

ha yew lo lo lo ha yaw lo lo lo o o lo lo lo lo si

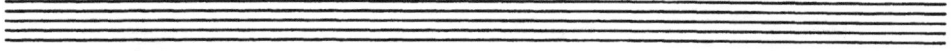

e e e hey hey

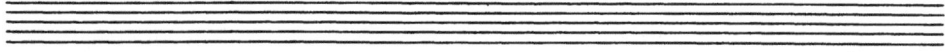

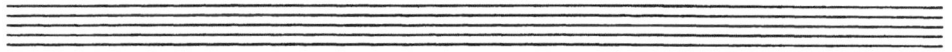

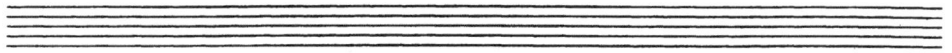

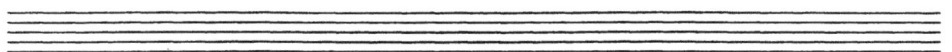

Figure 54. Performances of Phrase A

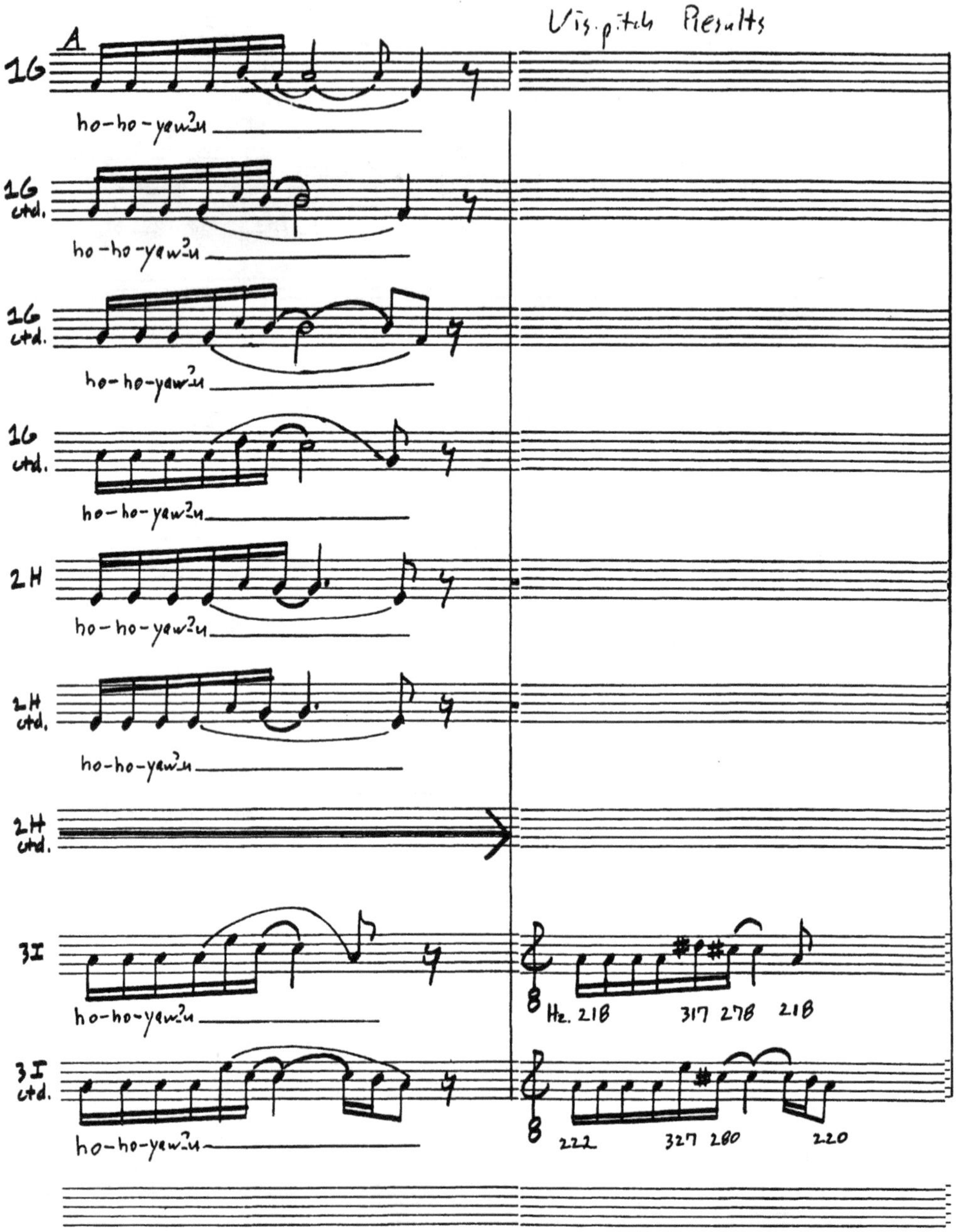

Figure 54. *(Continued)*

reminded that the renditions do not occur simultaneously but are placed one above another for purposes of comparison. In this case the lines and spaces represent those of the treble, rather than the bass, clef. Performances by both men and women sound an octave lower than written. Due to the number of staves required, the performances of the men are given on the left-hand pages, those of the women on the right. Singers H and I do not sing an Initial Refrain, so transcriptions of their renditions begin later in the figure. In some statements of the lullaby only two central phrases are sung rather than three and the Following Refrain is sung immediately after the second central phrase, or the phrases are sung out of their usual order. In such cases an arrow is drawn in all staves not involved in a given phrase to indicate that they continue on to the next transcribed phrase. Only singers H and K sing a section of vocables following a statement of the lullaby. Thus they are the only singers represented in the last part of Figure 53.

4.5. Comparison of the Melodies

The capital letters found above the staves represent the contour analysis. For purposes of clarity, a period is placed after the analysis of each contour. In the statements of the lullaby transcribed, each singer consistently employs the same contour in singing phrases A, B, and C. Singer G performs the contour M H L and the other five singers the contour L H L. Although all singers but G make use of the same contour, the intervallic relationships are not necessarily the same.

In Figure 54 I offer transcriptions of all performances of phrase A. With 11 of these are associated pitches derived acoustically from the Visipitch fundamental analyzer and their Hz. numbers (see 2.1.4, and Fig. 6). The recordings of singers G and H were old and the noise level was too great to permit analysis by the Visipitch. Of the singers who sing more than one repetition of the song in a given performance, only H and I reasonably maintain both contour and pitch level. Singers G and L raise their pitch level as they progress from one statement of the lullaby to another. This is reflected in the level of the transcribed phrases of singer G. However, the rise in pitch of singer L is less prominent. In most cases it is only the melodic contour which is stable. As mentioned previously (2.1.4), my transcriptions made by ear vary occasionally from the pitches derived from the Visipitch.

While the Hopi may conceive their melodies as a series of contours, this does not mean that they do not recognize melodic differences. After singer J had sung the lullaby, I played for her the recorded performance of G. I then asked her if she had sung the same words and the same melody. She replied that the words were the same but that her melody differed somewhat from that of the other singer. The two transcriptions in question are 1G and 4J in Figure 53. It can be seen that the words he sang are indeed the same except for the number of repetitions of *puwva* in the refrain. The contours of both refrain and phrases differ in the two performances.

In Figure 55 I offer the totals of the various contours employed in the performances of the lullaby.

Figure 55. Totals of Contours Employed in the Lullaby

Contour	Refrain	Phrases
H L M	17	0
M H L	4	12
L H L	0	36
H L H	9	0
H L	6	0
L H M	0	2

The two occurrences of L H M are caused by the singer running out of breath before she finished the phrase. It can thus be said that this contour was not produced intentionally. Thus, in reality, only two contours are employed in singing phrases A, B, and C. These two, of course, are very much alike.

4.6. The Sung Texts

In Figure 56 I give all performances of the text as sung. The formal analysis is placed to the left of the text. IR and FR represent Initial Refrain and Following Refrain, respectively. The three central phrases are identified as A, B, and C, since they are most frequently sung in this order. V represents a series of vocables or meaningless syllables. Two versions of phrase B are in common use. I have labeled these B^1 and B^2. As indicated previously, Hopi words are usually combinations of more than one grammatical element such as a noun and its possessive pronoun. The word or prefix *su* may be translated as "exactly." When it is present, it signifies that the beetles are found in the middle of the road. When it is absent, the meaning is that the beetles are found elsewhere on the trail or near it. The final *u* of phrases A and C, according to Malotki, is not a vocable but a pausal suffix. This suffix can be added

Figure 56. The Sung Texts of the Lullaby

Performance 1G

IR	puwva puwva puwva puwva puwva puwva
A	hohoyaw·u
B^1	supööpave'e
C	naa·iikwi·ukyang·u
IR	puwva puwva puwva puwva puwva puwva
A	hohoyaw·u
B^1	supööpave'e
C	naa·iikwi·ukyang·u
IR	puwva puwva puwva puwva puwva puwva
A	hohoyaw·u
B^1	supööpave'e
C	naa·iikwi·ukyang·u
IR	puwva puwva puwva puwva puwva
A	hohoyaw·u
B^1	supööpave'e
C	naa·iikwi·ukyang·u
FR	puwva puwva puwva puwva puwva puwva

Performance 2H

A	hohoyaw·u
C	naa·iikwi·ukyang·u
FR	puwva puwva puwva puwva
V	zei zei zei zei zei zei zei zei zei zei zei zei zei zei zei zei zei zei zei zei zei zei zei zei zei
A	hohoyaw·u
C	naa·iikwi·ukyang·u
B^1	shupööpave'e
FR	Puwva puwva puwva puwva
V	zei zei zei zei zei zei zei zei zei zei zei zei zei zei zei zei zei zei zei zei zei zei zei zei
B^1	shupööpave'e
C	naa·iikwi·ukyang·u
FR	puwva puwva puwva puwva

Performance 3I

A	hohoyaw·u
B^1	shupööpave'e
C	naa·iikwi·uchang·u
FR	puwva puwva ye puwva puwva
A	hohoyaw·u
B^1	shupööpave'e
C	naa·iikwi·uchang·u
FR	puwva puwva ye puwva puwva puwva (spoken:) he puwva

Performance 4J

IR	puwva'ha puwva puwva'ha'ha puwva
A	hohoyaw·u
B^1	supööpave'e
C	naa·iikwi·ukyang·u
FR	puwva'ha puwva'ha puwva

Performance 5K

IR	puwva puwva'a puwva
A	hohoyaw·u
B^2	pööpave'e
C	naa·iikwi·ukyang·u
FR	puwva'a puwva puwva
V	ha yew lo lo lo ha yaw lo lo lo o o lo lo lo lo lo si a a a ha e e e hey hey

Figure 56. *(Continued)*

Performance 6K

IR   puwva puwva'a puwva puwva
A   hohoyaw'u
B^2 pööpave'e
C   naa'iikwi'ukyang'u
FR   puwva'a puwva puwva puwva puwva'a puwva puwva

Performance 7K

IR   puwva puwva'a puwva
A   hohoyaw'u
B^2 pööpave'e
C   naa'iikwi'ukyang'u
FR   puwva'a puwva puwva puwva puwva'a puwva puwva

Performance 8K

IR   puwva puwva puwva
A   ohoyaw'u
B^2 pööpave'e
C   naa'iikwi'ukyang'u
FR   puwva'a puwva puwva puwva puwva'a puwva puwva

Performance 9L

IR   puwva puwva puwva puwva puwva'a'a'a puwva
A   hohoyaw'u
C   naa'iikwi'ukyang'u
FR   puwva'a puwva

Performance 10L

IR   puwva puwva puwva puwva
A   hohoyaw'u
C   naa'iikwi'ukyang'u
FR   puwva'a puwva
IR   puwva puwva puwva puwva puwva puwva
A   hohoyaw'u
C   naa'iikwi'ukyang'u
B^2 pööpave'e
FR   puwva'a puwva

Performance 11L

IR   puwva puwva puwva
A   hohoyaw'u
B^2 pööpave'e
C   naa'iikwi'ukyang'u
FR   puwva puwva'a puwva puwva

in certain circumstances at the end of a word before a pause. It is not obligatory but it is commonly used, especially in singing.

4.7. Comparison of the Sung Texts

Each of these text transcriptions represents a single discrete performance, which may include as many as four repetitions of the entire lullaby without pause. As can be seen there is considerable variation in the sung text. Some of these variations are minute and consist only of the addition, repetition, or substitution of certain phones. In all performances of B^1 or B^2 the final vowel, e, is repeated as a breath accent. Similar breath accents are found following the final a of *puwva* and can be seen in both the Initial and Final Refrains of performances 4J and 5K as well as in other performances by the latter singer. In performance 4J the aspiration h is added to the breath accent. Thus in performances by K one finds *puwva'a* and in that by J *puwva'ha'ha*. As indicated previously, the Hopi s lies somewhere between our s and sh. In each case I have written the version indicated by my ear. Finally, in performance 3I, in the last free form of phrase C, ch is substituted for the ky commonly spoken or sung. This is apparently an aspect of dialect of the Second Mesa.

For the purpose of analysis, I first establish the parameters of a single statement of the song. I consider this to consist of a minimum of two phrases, one of which is C, and at least one group of *puwva*s in the form of a refrain. As indicated, in some performances only one statement of the lullaby is heard while in others as many as four may be sung without interruption. These repetitions may or may not be exact. Five of the singers sang the song more than once in one or several performances. Of these five only singer G sang the same text throughout, both refrain and phrases.

4.7.1. Variation in the Refrain

The greatest variation is seen in the refrain. Of the five singers who sang the song more than once, only two, G and H, consistently sang the same number of *puwva*s in each refrain. Figure 57 lists the various forms of the refrain and the number of times each occurs. When there are two groups of *puwva*s in the

Figure 57. Number of *Puwva*s in Refrains and Their Groupings

Repetitions of *Puwva*	Occurrences
2	3
2 + 2	2
2 + 3	1
2 + 4	1
3	6
3 + 3	7
3 + 4	1
4	4
5	1

refrain—the division is established by the occurrence of a breath—they are connected with a plus sign.

4.7.2. Variation in the Non-Refrain Portions of the Texts

Variation in the formal organization of the non-refrain section of the text is not as great. It should be remembered that the three phrases were assigned the letters A, B, and C since this is the most common order in which they occur and that the two forms of phrase B are alike except for the presence or absence of the initial prefix su or shu. In Figure 58 I list the various forms taken by the non-refrain section of the text and the number of occurrences of each.

Figure 58. Variation in Non-Refrain Portion of Text

Order of Phrases	Occurrences
AB^1C	7
AB^2C	5
ACB^1	1
ACB^2	1
AC	3
B^1	1

The interchange of phrases B and C seems very common. After recording performances 4J and 5K, I asked each singer to speak rather than sing the text of the song. In doing so, both singers spoke the central phrases in the order ACB rather than ABC. I asked the Hopi who was translating for me to listen to performance 4J and to speak the words of the song. He also reversed the order, saying the phrases in the order ACB rather than ABC. Obviously it is important to know that the creature referred to is a beetle and that it is carrying another on its back. Where it and the beetle it is carrying are located in relationship to the trail or road can be added later, as in form ACB, or omitted, as in form AC. I doubt if the form BC would occur unless phrase A had been sung earlier, as it is in performance 3H.

Chapter 5 Stability and Variation

5.1. Variation in Time and Space

The performances transcribed represent some variety in both time and space. The kachina dance songs were recorded in three different time periods and represent two areas of the Hopi Reservation. The lullabies were recorded during four time periods and represent three areas of the Reservation. The sample is too small to permit the establishment of stylistic differences of performances of the songs in different areas of the Reservation and the changes which have occurred in time. However, there is some evidence concerning such differences which should be considered.

5.1.1. In the Kachina Dance Song

The kachina dance song is sufficiently different in the performances at the First and Third Mesas that a separate text be provided for each. The repetition of segment Z and of the Moccasin may be a Third Mesa tradition since no Hopi at the First Mesa mentioned this possibility. Figure 59 contrasts the pitch contours of all performances sung at the First Mesa in 1960 with Performance 1A, sung at the First Mesa in 1926, and performance 8F, sung by a Third Mesa singer in 1984.

In the below figure the first column represents the segments. The second column offers the contours commonly sung in all performances by the First Mesa singers except A. The third column gives the ratio at which this contour was sung, the figure to the right of the slash representing the total number of performances of the segment, the left figure the number of times the contour was sung. The remaining columns contrast the performance by A and the three parts of the performance by F. If either A or F agree with the majority of the First Mesa singers, a *Y* is placed in the appropriate column. If there is no agreement, there is an *N* in the column. Should either A or F not sing a particular segment, nothing is placed in the column.

Although approximately 36 years separate the performance by 1A in 1924 and the remainder of the First Mesa performances in 1960, there is an average agreement between them of 93 percent. On the other hand, the Third Mesa singer is in agreement with the First Mesa majority only 76 percent of the time. This figure is slightly above the established norm but would seem to indicate a different concept of the melody at the Third Mesa. However, the Third Mesa singer, who said he learned the song from his grandmother, had not been active in Hopi ceremonial life for 20 years before he sang the song. The evidence therefore is not strong.

5.1.2. In the Lullaby

The versions of the lullaby sung by the women from the First Mesa, singers J, K, and L, have one characteristic in common. This might be described as the performance of a melodic circumflex extending the second syllable of the word *puwva*. Three examples are given in Figure 60.

Lullaby 2H was sung by a Navaho rather than by a Hopi at a site off the Hopi Reservation. Nevertheless, performance 2H is similar in a number of respects to performance 3I from Shipaulovi, Second Mesa. The characteristics they have in common are 1) no refrain precedes the first statements of the phrases; 2) the Following Refrain consists of one group of 4-5 *puwva*s; and 3) a tremolo-like effect is employed in singing the first *puwva* of the refrain. Examples of this are offered in Figure 61.

The 1903 recording made at the Third Mesa ca. 1903 is primarily differentiated from the performances at the two other mesas by the contour with which the phrases are sung. Since I have only one example from the Third Mesa and there is a 50E year lapse of time between this recording and the next recording of the lullaby in 1956, it is impossible to determine whether this is a stylistic characteristic of the Third Mesa or a form which has been modified in later use.

Figure 59. Comparison of Contours Sung in Performances 1A and 8F with
Contours Sung by the Majority of the Remaining First Mesa Singers (B-E)

Segment	Contour sung by Majority of First Mesa Singers (Except A)	Ratio of Agreement	1A	8Fa	8Fb	8Fc
A	H L H	5/7	N	N	N	
B	H L	7/7	Y	Y	N	
C	H L	6/6	Y	Y	Y	
D	M H L	6/6	Y	Y	N	
E	M H L	6/6	Y	Y	Y	
F	M H L	4/6	Y	Y	Y	
G	L H M	3/6	N	N	N	
H	H L	6/6	Y	N	Y	
I	H L	5/5	Y	Y	N	
J	H L	3/5	Y	Y	Y	
K	H L	4/6	Y	Y	Y	
L	H L	4/6	Y	Y	Y	
M	M H L	5/5	Y		Y	
N	M H L M	5/5	Y		Y	
O	H L	3/5	Y		Y	
P	M^2 H L M^1	6/6	Y		Y	
Q	H L	6/6	Y		Y	
R	H L H	5/5	Y		Y	
S	M H L	4/5	Y		N	
T	H L H	5/5	Y		Y	
U	H L H	5/5	Y		Y	
V	M H L M	3/5	Y		Y	
W	M H L	5/5	Y		Y	
X	H L M	5/5	Y		Y	
Y	H L H	5/5	Y		Y	
Z	M H L	5/5	Y		Y	Y
Moc. 1	M H L	5/5	Y		Y	Y
Moc. 2	M H L	4/5	Y		Y	Y
Moc. 3	M H L	5/5	Y		Y	Y
Moc. 4	H L	5/5	Y		N	N

Ratios of Agreement

1A	8Fa	8Fb	8Fc	Total for Singer F
28/30	9/12	23/30	4/5	36/47
93%	75%	76%	80%	76%

5.2. Summary Conclusions

5.2.1. Stability and Variation in the Texts

5.2.1.1. In the Kachina Dance Song

Considering the fact that the kachina dance song has been in the oral tradition for some time, the meaningful text is quite stable. The other Hopis who listened to performances of the song at my request found only one change in wording, this being a difference in number in a noun in the 1924 version as contrasted with that used in the remainder of the First Mesa performances. My second translator informed me that there was a Zuni word sung in the 1924 performance. The other Hopi who listened to this apparently assumed it to be vocables rather than a word.

There are further differences between the Third Mesa version (1984) and those of the First Mesa which the 1960 informants obviously could not have heard. One of these is the transposition of a word to a different place in the song, the second the substitution of an expletive for an honorific at the very beginning. Likewise the Third Mesa singer added to a word a particle which is not found in any of the First Mesa versions.

Figure 60. *Puwva* Configuration, First Mesa

Figure 61. *Puwva* Configuration, Second Mesa

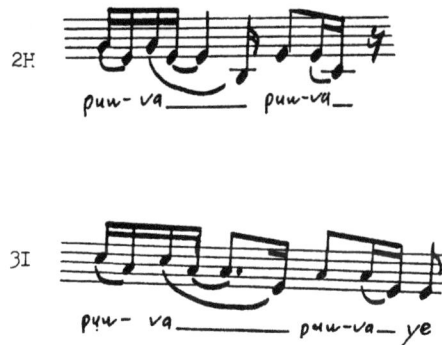

There are also a number of omissions of words in the sung performances. Some of these occur in 2Ba which was obviously curtailed by the singer as he was not satisfied with his performance. Singer D also omits two full free forms. This seems the only characteristic of his performance which would cause the Hopi to inform me that this man was a poor singer.

There are a few non-phonemic substitutions, elisions, or additions in the two contrasting spoken texts. These probably represent dialect differences or errors on the part of the singers. As previously indicated, the spoken texts are derived from the sung texts.

There are certain traditional ways in which the text can be lengthened. The first half of the song (I am referring to the A portion of the song, as the B section was not transcribed and was not recorded in most cases) can be repeated and the Moccasin lengthened. Another means of lengthening, which seems to be a Third Mesa tradition, consists of repeating segment Z and the Moccasin. Since all three are probably conventional, they do not affect the stability of the song. On the other hand, the song can be shortened by the omission of the Identificatory Introduction.

In most cultures there are some substitutions, elisions, or additions in singing as contrasted with what occurs when the same text is spoken. The percentage of these occurring in Hopi song does not seem to be unusually large, but the three most common types should be noted as acceptable variation. The most important of these is the substitution in singing of *ey* for the *i* of speech, which occurs a little over half of the time. Also frequently heard is the addition of *y* to the final *a* of a word. As indicated, glottal stops occurring between words are not written since they normally are required in spoken Hopi. However, it is interesting to note that in singing over two thirds of the glottal stops in the spoken text are not present. These three common modifications of the text are apparently acceptable within the parameters of variation. The first two, in fact, may form part of performance style.

The breath accent is a characteristic of the Hopi singing style. My analysis has caused me to amplify the meaning of the term to include extension by breath accent on a different vowel and on a different pitch. The first is fairly rare, the breath accent being sung on the same vowel 95 percent of the time. The percentage of breath accents sung on the same pitch as the syllable they follow is smaller. The movement is usually downward. The singers are not consistent as to when they extend a syllable by use of the breath accent nor by how many breath accents it is extended. This, again, seems to fall within the parameters of acceptable variation.

Neither is great consistency shown in the type or number of vocables sung in the first half of the song or in the Moccasin. Apparently, this type of variation, like that seen in the breath accents, is acceptable in individual performances of the song. I would assume that in performances in the plaza or the kiva the same number of breath accents and vocables would have to be sung in order to match the steps of the dance. I have no way of knowing if all singers would employ the same vowels and consonants. The Hopi do not allow recordings by others of their performances in the kiva or in the plaza. I was also refused permission to have a group of men rehearse a song and then be recorded singing it as a group. At ritual performances they sing through masks which interfere with clarity of both pronunciation and pitch.

The vocables of the Identificatory Introduction are much more regular, that is, there is much greater agreement among the singers. This is to be expected, since this group of vocables has a symbolic meaning.

5.2.1.2. In the Lullaby

The lullaby is much more varied in form than the longer kachina dance song. The three central phrases may be sung in more than one order, the refrain may contain a varied number of *puwvas*, and the song may begin either with the refrain or the phrases. Nevertheless, there is always sufficient textual content in each performance to identify the song. In determining the acceptable parameters of variation in the lullaby I distinguish three levels, the first the most stable, the third the least. At the first level I list those elements which are always present in any statement of the song. Two phrases are always present, one of which is C. To this is added a refrain consisting of not less than one group of *puwvas*. At the second level are meaningful text elements which may or may not be present in any performance of the song. Phrase A is almost always present, phrase B is frequently present in one of two alternative forms. The Initial Refrain is also more often present than not. At the third level I place the only element of this song which is subject to free variation, the section of vocables.

At the non-phonemic level there is only one substitution of phones, in the performance from the Second Mesa. This probably represents a difference in dialect. In addition, the First Mesa women singers introduce a small number of breath accents.

5.2.2. Stability and Variation in the Music

5.2.2.1. Assumptions Made in Transcribing and Analysing The Music

In analyzing the music of the songs I have made three assumptions: 1) the Hopi conceive their melodies in terms of contours rather than discrete pitches; 2) the pitch band notation I have developed as a method of transcribing these melodies is adequate to reflect these contours; 3) when three quarters of the performers are in agreement concerning any element being analyzed, this agreement can be considered to reflect a cultural norm.

5.2.2.2. In the Kachina Dance Song

In comparing the contours of the segments sung in the kachina dance song, not including the Identificatory Introduction, it was found that the performers were in average agreement 83 percent of the time. Another method of calculation produced a consensus of 87 percent.

Not all the singers perform the Identificatory Introduction. However, an analysis of the five performances heard indicates that the average of agreement is 85 percent. This is slightly lower than the 87 percent of the remainder of the contours but above the 83 percent of the first calculation. Since the contours of the Identificatory Introduction of the kachina dance song are symbolic of the kachina being represented, one would expect a higher percentage. If we had eight performances of the Identificatory Introduction to analyze, rather than only five, a higher average of agreement might have been secured.

It will be noted that considerable variation from our point of view can occur without the listening Hopi feeling that the song is not sung properly. If the Hopi's concept of song is that of a series of contours, it follows that he will have a different concept of pitch level. Thus in two performances by the same singer, the two melodic lines neither coincide nor remain consistently equidistant. Two of the performers sang the song twice. I therefore compare the two performances by the same singer to determine what his conception of pitch level is. These comparisons are somewhat complicated by the fact that singer B in his first performance did not complete the first half of the song, but tacked on the closing vocables, returned to the first segment, and then sang through the song. The first comparison of performances by the same singers dealt with the intervals occurring at the beginning and end of the segments and the largest interval found within the segments. Since the pitch band is a whole tone in width, it can contain two minor seconds.

In assessing the average of agreement in pitch level I have therefore combined the instances of occurrence of intervals of the unison and the second. When, in two performances by the same singer, one is running approximately a second higher than the other, it is transposed down so that a more adequate comparison can be made. When performances 6C/3C are compared they are more consistent in pitch level than performances 7B/2Bb and 2Ba/2Bb. In 6C/3C the agreement is 92 percent, in 7B/2Bb 78 percent, and in 2Ba/2Bb 67 percent. The first is high above the norm, the second exceeds the norm, and the third is below it. A reassessment of the results analyzing only those segments sung in all performances, that is, omitting those in which 2Ba is not represented, does not materially alter the results achieved.

In comparing performances by the same singer, another means of assessing pitch level is to compare the interval found between the end of one segment and the beginning of a subsequent segment. A comparison of melographs made of two performances by the same singer demonstrates that this interval does not always remain constant. In this analysis one interval represents the connection of the two segments. However, as before, due to the exigencies of the pitch band notation, seconds and unisons are combined. In performances 6C/3C the average of agreement is 92 percent; the average of agreement between 7B and 2Bb is 86 percent. Performances 2Ba/2Bb represent less than half of the song. As usual, analysis of its intervals produces an average agreement lower than the norm.

In comparing two performances by the same singer the pitch level relationship between two adjacent contours sometimes varies by as much as a third. Variations of a second are common. This flexibility in pitch relationship is quite contrary to practice in Western tradition, as is the fact that the Hopi take breaths within words when singing.

These analyses of pitch levels strengthen three conclusions previously made on the basis of other evidence, as stated in Chapter 3 (3.8.2). These are: 1) singer C is somewhat more consistent at maintaining an established pitch level than singer B; 2) both singers find it easier to maintain the established pitch level in the second section of the song than in the first; 3) performance 2Ba remains less consistent than the others, thus strengthening my belief that singer B did not find this portion of his performance adequate.

5.2.2.3. In the Lullaby

Turning to the melodies of the lullabies I again distinguish three levels, the first the most stable, the third the least. At the first level I list those elements of melody which are always present in this song. Melodically the initial motion of the phrase contours is ascending. In contrast, the initial motion of the refrain contours is descending. The second level consists of melodic elements which are always present in one or more alternative forms. Thus the melodic contour to which a group of *puwva*s is sung may continue to descend, or may ascend to the initial pitch or an intermediate pitch. Three alternative contours are produced. In contrast, the pitch con-

tours of the phrases, after leaping upward, return to the pitch at which they began or to a pitch just below it. Thus two alternative contours are produced. In the third level I again place that element of the song which may be sung to any series of contours that the singer may elect, the section of vocables.

5.3. Comparison with Song in Our Culture

The text of a Hopi song seems, in general, to be less stable than that of a song of our culture. Repetitions of a section of the text, as in the kachina dance song, are common in our song. However, the transposition of a word or statement, as in *tawanita*, from one position in the text to another is not likely. Nor in our culture does the singer commonly at will omit the first portion of a song, as the Identificatory Introduction in the kachina dance song and the Initial Refrain in the lullaby. The admonition to the child to go to sleep might be repeated an uneven number of times in one of our lullabies but this would probably occur at a specific point in the song, as at its close. Certainly a change in the order in which the textual phrases of the song are sung would be quite unusual. Nonsense syllables occur in the texts of our songs but do not form as important a component as in the Hopi repertory. When they do occur in our song they are likely to be repeated exactly while the Hopi allow a good deal of variation or even improvisation. Thus when compared with the body of our own song, the texts of those of the Hopi are considerably more flexible in their organization. Nevertheless, there is ample content in each song, as well as sufficient chronology in which its parts are sung, to establish its identity.

If the assumptions underlying the analysis of the music and the methods employed in this analysis be accepted, it can be said that Hopi melody is reasonably stable, but not necessarily in the sense that we view our own music. Hopi music is not based on a fixed scale derived from the playing of musical instruments. From our point of view, the Hopi accepts a considerable amount of variation. The stability seen is based upon similarity rather than precise identity. Again, from our point of view, one might almost say that it is based on gross similarities only. Nevertheless, there is sufficient likeness in contour, pitch level, and form to identify the kachina dance song and the lullaby as two particular songs which will immediately be recognized as such by any Hopi hearing them.

Appendix:
Guide to Hopi Pronunciation

This guide was adapted from P. David Seaman's *Hopi Dictionary* (1985). It is used by kind permission of Professor Seaman. Changes made in his system are noted. The English equivalents for the Hopi phone clusters *ngw* and *ngy* were suggested by Robert Austerlitz. For further information see 2.2.6, Pronunciation and Orthography, p. 00.

Phoneme	English Equivalent
a	f<u>a</u>ther
e	p<u>e</u>p
h	<u>h</u>it
i	mach<u>i</u>ne
k	s<u>k</u>ill
ky	<u>c</u>ue
kw	<u>qu</u>ail
l	<u>l</u>ook
m	<u>m</u>ain
n	<u>n</u>ail
ng	so<u>ng</u>
ngw	lo<u>ng w</u>alk
ngy	lo<u>ng y</u>am
ö	(none—see Additional Pronunciation Hints following) Seaman uses the *ø*, as in Danish, to represent this phoneme.
o	h<u>o</u>pe
p	<u>p</u>ill
q	<u>c</u>aught
qw	<u>qu</u>ote
r	a<u>z</u>ure
s	between <u>s</u>ee and <u>sh</u>e
t	s<u>t</u>ill
ts	se<u>ts</u>
u	p<u>u</u>t
v	<u>v</u>ail
w	<u>w</u>ill
y	<u>y</u>ou

Phoneme	English Equivalent
'	oh_oh Seaman uses the apostrophe, rather than the raised comma, to represent the glottal stop. (I have used the apostrophe to represent the breath accent—see 2.2.7., p. 00.)

Additional Pronunciation Hints

ö	This Hopi vowel is similar to the *e* in English "met," except that the lips are rounded. I consider the sound to be somewhat related to the *ö* in German.
q	This consonant is like a *k* sound, but is made with the tongue lightly touching the back of the throat.
r	The Hopi *r* is nothing like an English *r*; rather it is something like an English *z* or *zh* but with the tongue tip curled back a little.
u	Unlike English, the Hopi *u* is usually made with unrounded lips.
v	The Hopi *v* is often pronounced with the lower lip vibrating against the upper lip instead of against the upper teeth as in English.
'	The glottal stop is like a catch in the throat.
p,t,k,q	These stops are voiceless and unaspirated in Hopi. As in Spanish, there is no puff of air after these phonemes.

Length

Hopi vowels may be either short or long in duration. Vowel length is indicated by doubling the vowel, e.g., *pep*, "there," and *peep*, "almost." The sound difference is equivalent to the difference in duration of the English *e* in "bet" vs. "bed," except that in Hopi this small difference in pronunciation causes a change in meaning, as just illustrated

Bibliography

Black, Robert A.
1964   "A Content Analysis of 81 Hopi Indian Chants." Ph.D. dissertation, Indiana University. Ann Arbor: University Microfilms.

Colton, Harold F.
1949   *Hopi Kachina Dolls*. Albuquerque: University of New Mexico Press.

Curtis, Natalie
1907   *The Indian's Book*. Reprint, NY: Dover Publications, Inc., 1968.
1921   "American Indian Cradle Songs." *Musical Quarterly* 7:549-58.

Earle, Edwin and Edward A. Kennard
1938   *Hopi Kachinas*. New York: J. J. Augustin.

Frisbie, Charlotte J.
1977   *Music and Dance Research of Southwestern United States Indians*. Detroit Studies in Music Bibliography, No. 36. Detroit: Information Coordinators, Inc.

Gilman, Benjamin
1891   "Zuni Melodies." *Journal of American Ethnology and Archaeology* 1:63-91.
1908   "Hopi Songs." *Journal of American Ethnology and Archaeology* 5:1-226.

Kealiinohomoku, Jean
1967   "Hopi and Polynesian Dance: A Study in Cross-Cultural Comparisons." *Ethnomusicology* 11:343-58.

Kennard, Edward A.
1948   *Little Hopi*. Phoenix: U. S. Indian Service, Phoenix Indian School.

List, George
1962   "Song in Hopi Culture, Past and Present." *Journal of the International Folk Music Council* 14:30-35.
1963   "An Approach to the Indexing of Ballad Tunes." *The Folklore and Folk Music Archivist* 6 (1): 7-16.
1964   "The Hopi and the White Man's Music." *Sing Out* 14 (2): 47, 49.

1968   "The Hopi as Composer and Poet." In *Proceedings of the Centennial Workshop in Ethnomusicology*, held at the University of British Columbia 19-23 June 1967. Ed. Peter Crossley-Holland. Vancouver: Government of the Province of British Columbia. Pp. 43-53.
1974   "The Reliability of Transcription." *Ethnomusicology* 18:353-77.
1983   *Music and Poetry in a Colombian Village: A Tri-Cultural Heritage*. Bloomington: Indiana University Press.
1985   "Hopi Melodic Concepts." *Journal of the American Musicological Society* 38:143-52.
1987   "Stability and Variation in a Hopi Lullaby." *Ethnomusicology* 31:18-34.

MacLeish, Kenneth
1941   "A Few Hopi Songs from Moenkopi." *Masterkey* 15:178-84.

Malotki, Ekkehart
1979   *Hopi-Raum: eine sprachwissenschaftliche Analyse der Raumvorstellungen in der Hopi-Sprache*. Tübingen: TBL Verlag Gunter Narr.

Rhodes, Robert W.
1973   "Selected Hopi Secular Music: Transcription and Analysis." Ed.D. dissertation, Arizona State University. Ann Arbor: University Microfilms.
1977   *Hopi Music and Dance*. Tsaile, AZ: Navajo Community College Press.

Seaman, P. David
1985   *Hopi Dictionary*. Northern Arizona University Anthropological Paper No. 2. Flagstaff: Northern Arizona University Press.

Voegelin, C.F. and F.M. Voegelin
1957   *Hopi Domains: a lexical approach to the problem of selection*. Supplement to *International Journal of American Linguistics* 23(2). Reprint, Chicago: University of Chicago Press, 1974.

Index

amplitude 6, 8, 18
appoggiatura 8

Black, Robert 3
breathing 8, 15
  accents 8, 15, 16, 18, 20, 24, 43n, 55, 64, 65-69, 93, 97

chant and song 4
contour 6, 8, 10, 11, 12, 13, 14, 44, 46, 47, 90, 96, 99
  analysis 6, 13, 14, 26, 44, 45, 56, 90
Curtis, Natalie 2, 14

Dances
  Basket 2
  Butterfly 2
  Home 21
  Kachina 1, 2, 21
    costume 22-23
    description 21
    melody range 11
  Rainbow 2
  Snake 1, 2

Ekstrom, Jonathan O. 15, 17
elision 26, 27, 63-64

Fewkes, J. Walter 2, 3

Gilman, Benjamin 3, 5
glides 13
glottal stop 17, 18, 19, 58, 63, 97
Great Black Mesa 1

Hano 1
Hodge, Carleton 15, 16, 17
Hopi
  ceremony 1
    Powamu 1, 2, 21
  language 1
    spoken 4, 15
    sung 4, 15
  men 1, 21, 22
  society 1
  Tribal Council 3
  women 1, 21

Kakapti 2, 15, 23
Kivas 1, 21

lullabies 1, 12, 77-92 passim, 95, 98, 99
  black beetle 77
  refrain 93, 95
  Stink Beetle 3
  Stinkbug 3

Malotki, Ekkehart 16, 17, 25n
manas 21
Melographs 5, 6, 7, 10, 11, 12, 51, 99
Mocassin 44, 50-51, 53, 54, 55, 56, 69, 71, 72, 73, 74, 95, 97
"mudheads" 21

Navaho 3

Parks, Douglas 16, 17
phones 15, 16, 17, 25n, 26, 58, 63. 65
pitch 5, 6, 7, 8, 10, 11, 12, 13, 18, 46, 47-56 passim, 95, 98
pitch band notation 5, 6, 7, 47, 53, 98, 99
Plains-Pueblo 8

range 5
Rhodes, Robert W. 3

scale 3, 5
schwa 17
Seaman, P. David 4, 15, 16, 17, 25n
Sichomovi 1
singing style described 65
songs
  composition 5, 22
  disparities in versions 9, 26
  free form 6, 8, 24, 25n, 26, 43n, 56-57, 61n
  Kachina dance 2, 5, 10, 11, 12, 15, 17, 18, 21-75 passim, 95, 96
    Identificatory Introduction 5, 22, 27, 44, 46
    longhaired 2, 22
      barefoot longhaired 23, 44
    See lullabies
    transcription 6
Spaniards 1

tonality 3
transcription 3, 10, 12, 13-20 passim

vocables 5, 14, 15, 16, 22, 25n, 27, 43n, 69-75
Voegelin, Charles 15
Voegelin, Florence 15

Walpi 1
Whorf, Benjamin 4, 15

www.ingramcontent.com/pod-product-compliance
Lightning Source LLC
Chambersburg PA
CBHW061756260326
41914CB00006B/1124